American Jap Girl

A Samurai Daughter's Ikigai—
From Incarceration to Legacy

Richard Y. Okumoto

American Jap Girl
A Samurai Daughter's Ikigai—From Incarceration to Legacy

Publisher's Cataloging-in-Publication
(Provided by Cassidy Cataloguing Services, Inc.)

Names: Okumoto, Richard Y., author.
Title: American Jap girl : a samurai daughter's ikigai--from incarceration
    to legacy / Richard Y. Okumoto.
Description: Newport Beach, California : Digital Lifestory Press, [2026]
    | Includes index.
Identifiers: LCCN: 2025927889 | ISBN: 9781971076010 (paperback) |
    9781971076027 (hardcover) | 9781971076003 (ebook)
Subjects: LCSH: Okumoto, Tome. | Japanese American women--Bi-
    ography. | Women prisoners--United States--Biography.
    | Japanese Americans--Ethnic identity. | Japanese Ameri-
    cans--Civil rights. | Treaty of Versailles (1919 June 28) | Race
    discrimination--United States. | United States--Race rela-
    tions--History--20th century. | LCGFT: Biographies. | BISAC:
    BIOGRAPHY & AUTOBIOGRAPHY / Personal Memoirs. |
    SOCIAL SCIENCE / Ethnic Studies / Asian American Studies.
    | SOCIAL SCIENCE / Women's Studies.
Classification: LCC: E184.J3 O48 2026 | DDC: 305.488956073--dc23

Publication managed by AuthorImprints.com

Table of Contents

Author's Note

This memoir—the story of Tome (toh-meh)—originated from a promise. Shortly after her passing in 2004, I collected her handwritten journals and memoir notes, resurrected my memories from our conversations spanning thousands of hours, and met with her best friend, Mary (Uyeda) Maruyama. Surrounded by this material, I sat overwhelmed. To deliver on my promise, I spent the next twenty-one years preparing myself to fully understand and tell her story.

While pursuing my studies as a qualitative researcher, I collected the tools and skills necessary to listen deeply, code thematically, and synthesize meaningfully. The expertise I gained while earning my PhD enabled me to grasp the depth and complexity of her story, while my heart enabled me to interpret her life. Applying the principles of narrative inquiry, life history, and cultural phenomenology, I realized Tome's life story was both a personal memoir and a living case study of resilience, survival, maternal love, and identity.

Three unifying and consistent themes prevail in *American Jap Girl*: *ikigai* (ee-kee-GAH-ee), reflecting Tome's purpose in life, *Bushido* (boo-SHEE-doh), a moral set of principles historically followed by the samurai class in Japan, and *Kintsugi* (KIN-tsu-gee), where brokenness is embraced, creating dignity and beauty from a fractured whole. There is no one agreed-upon list of Bushido principles; the list that *American Jap Girl* follows is consistent with Dr. Nitobe Inazote's.

Tome and I lived *American Jap Girl* and shared its challenges and questions. For example, I was curious as to how and why we always felt socially inferior to Westerners. Why did we feel less than, no matter what our elders told us? Was there a historical inflection point that drove this into our psyches? One year before Tome passed, our conversations uncovered a deeper understanding of this topic. From a book in Tome's bookcase, Margaret MacMillan's *Paris 1919*, which gives an account of the Paris Peace Conference leading up to the completion of the Treaty of Versailles in 1919, we learned that conversations at the conference ended in a revelatory inaction: Japanese diplomats' requests for inclusion of a racial-equality paragraph in the Treaty of Versailles were rejected. This sparked among the Japanese a pivotal emotional explosion that may have cost more lives than the atomic bombs dropped during World War II—and had that paragraph been adopted, the bombings most likely would have been unnecessary. *American Jap Girl*'s story exposes to the world the possible consequences of the Paris Peace Conference events and the view held by key Western nations that the Japanese were inferior. Specifically, Tome's memoir shares how that one decision to omit the racial-equality paragraph in 1919 may have created an intergenerational impact on the Japanese people, which included my foster grandfather, my mom, and me.

Regarding tone, in the title and in several places within this memoir, I include words that are no longer used as they have been deemed derogatory, such as *Jap* for "Japanese" or *Oriental* for "Asian." These words were commonplace and reflect the tenor of the time periods discussed in this memoir.

A prime example is General DeWitt's 1940s comment: "A Jap is a Jap," whether a US citizen or not. President Roosevelt authorized him to forcibly relocate West Coast Japanese Americans through the power of the February 19, 1942, signing of Executive Order 9066. This attitude was not limited to those in positions of power; everyday individuals displayed similar sentiments on large, posted signs: JAPS KEEP MOVING . . . THIS IS A WHITE MAN'S NEIGHBORHOOD.

Cesar Chavez is credited with saying, "You can't humiliate someone who has pride." His belief is upheld in this memoir: Through her strength, derived from Bushido, Tome reclaims the slur *Jap* or *Jap girl* and transforms it into a symbol of dignity and legacy. Tome did not just accept the moniker; she embraced it, refusing to let it silence her.

These elements are not unrelated anecdotes; they represent Tome's experiences that are emotionally and thematically coded through the vivid storytelling in *American Jap Girl*. With her passing, the story had to be told posthumously through her perspective—only Tome can tell this story with the authentic resonance of her legacy. While this literary framing is risky, I felt it necessary to project the power of her lived experience. The inclusion of my letters, journals, and telephone calls is a literary technique, the epistolary method, to insert my personal thoughts and dialogue without disrupting or interfering with Tome's narrative. Apart from the epilogue, this story is told through Tome's voice.

Please note that historical references, public statements, broadcasts, and widely circulated quotations appear as part of the lived cultural record of the periods described and are presented for narrative context and not for scholarly adjudication. Interpretive connections—linking historical events, cultural philosophies, and intergenerational consequence—reflect my own synthesis as a qualitative researcher and are informed by, but not dependent upon, existing historical scholarship.

American Jap Girl is the spiritual incarnation of Tome. Her one wish—that everyone would find a balanced humanity, an authentic reciprocity of respect and friendship—is infused throughout every page of this memoir. Her *ikigai* lives on in my heart, and in the heart of every reader.

Richard Y. Okumoto, PhD

Letter to the Reader

Tome realizes late in adolescence that her appearance will always be that of a Jap girl. This painful revelation brings a disturbing awareness that she is a perpetual foreigner and a visual immigrant in the eyes of America. Accepting this, Tome focuses on allowing her *ikigai* and world events to shape her personal choices in supporting her husband and guiding her children. She understands that having an *ikigai*, which may or may not change over a lifetime, is not enough. What is important to her is actualizing it every day to bring her joy.

Part One introduces Tome and me, her son and fourth child. It then transports us to Tome's youth: her innocence, her naïveté, and the childhood adversities she overcomes. Then, soon after she leaves behind her adolescence, a presidential decision destroys her constructed reality.

Part Two finds Tome, a United States citizen, incarcerated without legal due process at the age of twenty, based solely on her Japanese heritage. Tome is personally punished by the 1942 political administration's deceitful enactment of

Executive Order 9066, which ushers in a major violation of her civil rights as an American citizen and demolishes her protections under the Fifth Amendment of the United States Constitution. To allow them to stay together in the war camp, her foster father adopts her into his samurai family and gives her his name, Kawakita, and his legacy. (Historically, there were three paths to becoming samurai: birth, marriage, or adoption into a samurai family.)

While incarcerated, Tome becomes a young bride and births two daughters in a war camp on American soil. This experience fortifies Tome's character as she holds on to her dignity, demonstrates her personal resilience, and finds her *ikigai.* Tome's journey leads to the pure power of motherhood, where we begin to see her many diverse and complex layers. In her life post-incarceration, she faces and overcomes the challenges of poverty, motherhood, and racial discrimination. Painfully and sometimes comically exposed, her *ikigai* journey reveals her frailty, her sacrifice, her strength, her courage, and her hope.

Part Three intertwines Tome's story with mine, through letters, journals, and telephone calls. The last chapter brings closure to her life. In the epilogue, I bring closure to her *ikigai* gift to me and take steps to ensure her *ikigai* will live forever.

Tome's life as a visual immigrant in the eyes of America spans from the 1920s to the turn of the twenty-first century. It is set against the backdrop of the Great Depression, World War II and the atomic bomb, the Golden Age of America and the cultural revolution that followed, and the early Silicon Valley technology era of our nation. Throughout her journey, she created a balanced humanity in which there exists an authentic reciprocity of respect and friendship. Not only did she inspire and challenge me, through her lessons in Bushido, to find the same and achieve my dreams, she left a legacy of grace that promotes a culture of hope. Fractures in her life were repaired not by forgetting, but by honoring what was broken.

Tome often reminded me that there are no coincidences in life, just unrecognized patterns. Within her own life, I have discerned patterns that are embodied in this story—the story of Tome and me. Although samurai no longer exist, to me she will always be my Japanese American samurai.

Thanks, Mom.
Richard Y. Okumoto, PhD

Prologue

My Name Is Tome

On a brisk Southern California Sunday morning, one week after my eighty-second birthday, I sit up and take my last breath. My name is Tome, and within this moment of peace, my spirit bows before you and whispers, "Please, let me tell you my story...."

Although I come from a family of nine kids, I am given to another family, raised as an only child, schooled in Bushido. Later, I am adopted and become the daughter of a samurai. In my youth I sing, dance, and am an exceptional athlete. I grow up as the all-American farm girl, often seen running barefoot through open fields. I will miss that young girl whose dreams were shattered by life and world events but still found herself lifted up by hope and a sense of knowing. I will miss extending my dreams to my children, one generation away. I will miss being a wife, a mother, a sister, a good friend, an aunt, and a grandparent, surrounded by joy that was sometimes balanced by disappointments.

Basking in a bright light from above, I am caught between my old age and my youth—they form such a sharp contrast.

I see a sparkling pool of water reflecting a perfect image of my life. Slightly diffusing the bright light are blooming Sakura, cherry blossoms. Their short time to bloom mimics my short time to live. It is March 28, 2004, and I am falling backward onto the stark-white sheet on my cold hospital bed at Huntington Memorial in Pasadena. During my physical descent, I see the innocent face of my niece break into a waterfall of tears. Her husband, Ken, recently died at the age of sixty-two, a victim of colon cancer. Ken reaches out to me and lifts me above my deathbed and, reunited with him, I smile. My spirit floats above his widow and joins others who have passed before me. I no longer feel pain or struggle. I glance down at my physical body, which has landed softly onto the sheet and pillows. The bright light of life fades to a glimmer, illuminating what's left of me: a pale, frail, gaunt eighty-eight-pound woman.

With eyes closed and mind racing, I recall yesterday evening, my last night as a mother. I shared time and space with my son, Richard. He has four siblings and no children. His recent divorce, the death of his dad fourteen months ago, and now my passing will leave him orphaned. I have told Richard many times that my hope is that someone will be there to hold his hand and help him believe, believe in himself.

At fifty-two years of age, Richard will inherit my story through my journals, my notes, my imagination (based on our countless conversations), and my voice. Captured in these journals and notes are snippets of my life, from the age of twenty up until several weeks ago. These artifacts reveal fractures in my life mended with lines of dignity. He has promised to put them to good use. I know Richard will keep his promise, as he is my mystical child. He earned that honor through his actions in the fall of 1962.

Part One

Deconstructing My Reality

Throughout my childhood and adolescence, I saw myself as the all-American girl. I was a naïve, innocent child who found beauty and joy in running through open fields in Southern California. The first chapter in Part One introduces my mystical child. Following chapters capture my early life, beginning with my abandonment at three years old, when I was traded to another family like an unwanted pet. This, invited pain that became a periodic companion. It was during this time that relationships were built, trust was sometimes masked by silence, and I gained the emotional and physical strength to deal with fractures in my life—personal loss, polio, and the acceptance of how America sees me.

1

My Mystical Child

A mystical moment occurs in 1962. It starts with me sitting in our Southern California living room, watching a black-and-white television. The television is a gift to my husband, Set-chan, from a gardening customer. Many people refer to Set-chan as Charlie, as it is much easier to pronounce.

Suddenly, my heart stutters. It misses several steady beats. My chest tightens and nausea spreads throughout my body. My head bobs up, bringing my gaze into direct line of sight with the rabbit-ear antenna unit atop the faded and scratched television cabinet. For a moment I forget about my pain and giggle. The antenna reminds me of the coat-hanger Easter Bunny I once made for the kids. My eldest son stands up, walks to the television, and twists the antenna left, then right, jerking it back and forth in an attempt to improve the fuzzy television picture. Although I see no visible improvement, new trails of scratches are added to the top of the cabinet.

I sit upright on the dark-green paisley sofa, which is sticky from humidity and sweat. The residue of human toil has collected there, fogging what was once an unclouded plastic protective sofa cover. The stench cannot be erased from its slick surface. My eyes scan our living room, cloaked in depressing, faded lime-green paint; it reminds me of dried vomit, something I would avoid stepping on. The shredded curtains are closed, but they cannot suppress the dull-yellow glow emanating from the streetlight outside, casting shadows throughout the house. The bars on the windows and the solid-metal front door, protecting us from the dangers lurking outside, are constant reminders of our economic defeat. The house has been punished by the nine people who have lived in it: Set-chan and me, my foster parents, and my five kids.

Ba-bump, my heart stutters again. I need fresh air. I stand up and quietly leave the living room. I traverse the large kitchen with measured steps, struggling to carry one of the green kitchen-table chairs, and then haul it across the back porch and outside the house.

I must stop this pain.

Breathe.

I place the chair down and sit outside for a short respite, a moment of peace. From inside the house, deafening screams sully the pristine stillness of the evening. Set-chan's agonized howls are followed by distant crying. Piercing the dark, they remind me of the wounded wild animals I sometimes heard late at night while growing up on the chicken farm. In the morning, I would find them, half-eaten, with terrified expressions carved into their faces.

I close my eyes and hope that the fresh, cool night air might give me strength to persevere. Instead of achieving the desired sense of calm, I envision Set-chan's accident. I feel myself physically standing next to him, watching his legs being crushed between two cars. His screams of pain become my screams of pain, a torment we now both share. Helpless, I can do nothing. It is this recurring vision of his accident that adds anxiety to my daily fear, the fear of not being able to raise and feed my children after losing the family breadwinner.

I turn my eyes to the heavens and choke on a sky full of stars. The twinkling shimmers of distant radiance present a serene landscape that massages my troubled heart. I am reminded of evenings on the chicken farm when I was a child, sitting on my father's shoulders. I would sometimes reach up, hoping to clutch one star that might light my path through life. The chill of my cool, damp shirt brings me back to the present moment. I take another deep breath and slowly exhale. Vapor rises and scatters white clouds around my head.

A low-pitched, crackling sound gives me pause. Is there an animal in the darkness, ready to pounce on me? It quickly fades into a trickle and becomes a part of the night. As my eyes adapt to the dark, I see its source: a faint outline of water, catching streaks of light as it dances down concrete curvatures. As the sounds of the waterfall accompany the orchestrated night life surrounding me, I realize I am not alone.

Set-chan built a fishpond in our backyard, complete with a walking bridge and a waterfall. In the dark it resembles a Japanese picture postcard, a fantastical corner of our lives that preserves the honor and beauty of our exotic ancestors. In the daylight it is a shallow hole lined with cement and filled with stale water. Sitting in the dark, I smile, wishing our pond was the moat surrounding the Imperial Palace in Japan and I was the chosen one, or at least a member of the royal family.

The large fish occupying our pond are not regal koi, but instead mostly hearty goldfish who survive nocturnal raccoon attacks by hiding under the concrete bridge. Before each sunrise, several fragile fantail goldfish vanish, having provided a feast for these thieves of the dark. Sitting on flat stones surrounding the pond are croaking frogs the kids transplanted from Devil's Gate Dam, located next to the Jet Propulsion Laboratory here in Pasadena. The shiny skin of these repulsive creatures reflects the moonlight, displaying a green luminescence, adding depth and character to Set-chan's proud portrait of his Japanese ancestry.

Beyond the pond lies a small vegetable garden and a concrete slab that supports two metal T-framed hanging clotheslines. The absence of rain typically means newly washed clothes are pinned to this outdoor gallery, displaying our tattered shirts and pants. Wooden clothespins firmly secure our garments to the nylon lines and later prove to be great rubber band shooters for the kids. Hanging our clothes to dry is a chore I enjoy. It enables me to catch the warm rays of sunlight and watch the breeze effortlessly toss our rags back and forth. This airy lightness brings joy into my heart.

A prolonged silence follows. My attention is drawn away from the pond and diverted to the detached garage. I would like to say loud voices lead me to the garage, but there are none. I would like to say I am beckoned to the garage, but I am not. Deep inside my heart, I feel an uncontrollable urge drawing me toward it. I lean forward, stand up from my seated position, and slowly walk toward the garage, dragging my chair with me. The side door is partially open, and scattered light rays spill out of its dimly lit interior.

I gently push open the weather-beaten side door to its extreme limit, forming a large gateway through which I enter. The recent rain that has penetrated the interior garage beams produces a pungent, musty stench that adds to my discomfort. One side of the two-car garage is empty. I sold Set-chan's work truck to generate much-needed cash. The missing truck reinforces the loss of his financial support and heightens my fear of starvation and not being able to care for our children. Flashbacks of the World War II Japanese internment camps and our postwar resettlement torture me—the memories evoke deep emotional distress and hopelessness. I begin to choke, drowning in the large droplets that are forming a path from my eyes to my mouth. Fear grips me so tight, I can hardly breathe.

Following my instincts, I drag the kitchen chair into the center of the empty half of the garage. I walk over to a pile of Set-chan's tools and pick up one of his work ropes. I tie one end into a noose, something I learned how to do while growing up on the chicken farm. After several attempts, I successfully loft it over a thick crossbeam. I secure the straight end of the rope to a wall hook used for hanging Set-chan's gardening tools. I turn around, entranced by the swishing sound of the noose as it sways back and forth across the vacant half of the garage. Looking beyond the rope, I notice two standing rakes leaning against a crossbar. The shadowy image resembles a *torii* gate: a Japanese symbol defining entry into a divine space where peace may be found.

My breathing slows as my mind is quelled of panic and anxiety. I sense a *kami*—according to the Japanese Shinto religion, this may be a spiritual force, guiding me. Grabbing the noose, I step up and onto the green kitchen chair. I clumsily place the bristly rope around my neck. I pull on it to tighten its grip. As I look down, the snug-fitting rope pinches and chafes my neck. My feet in their scuffed, off-white work shoes stretch down, gripping and tearing the rolled ridge of the chair's seat cushion. At forty years old, I am standing at the precipice of life and death. I look straight forward and face the smirking shadow of the *Shinigami* (shee-nee-GAH-mee), the Japanese god of death. No words are spoken between us. I recognize him and understand his purpose.

As I edge off the end of the chair, my shoes squeak. The rope tightens around my neck, and I begin choking and coughing. My saliva mixes with my tears and drips to the concrete floor. I feel dampness on my legs as I lose control of my bodily functions.

My face feels slate gray, my eyes fill with more tears, and my lips quiver. The shadowy image of the *Shinigami* hovers around me. I desperately search for my final glimpse of life. Although I am silent, my head echoes with my screams for

Richard at ten years old

help. I am afraid to take my final decisive step. I am afraid to end it here.

At the sound of a terrified voice, I quickly look down, and the movement of my head tightens the rope around my neck. At this discomfort, I instinctively snap my head back to stop the choking. I catch a glimpse of my young son.

Standing above Richard, I see a brave child grab me and scream, "No, Mommy, no!"

A mere four feet tall, Richard holds me so tight, he cuts off the circulation to my lower body. His arms tremble, yet he does not let go. He does not run for help, he does not cry, he stands straight and acts.

Again, he shouts, "No, Mommy, no!"

His physical presence and strong words shock me into realizing what a horrible thing I am about to do to this innocent child. Through my tears, I catch a glimpse into the moral importance of my life to my ten-year-old son. His delicate and tiny form clinging to me saves me. My expression transforms from anguish and shame to purpose and remorse. Color returns and flushes my cheeks.

I slip off the noose—my escape and the representation of darkness in my life—from around my neck. I step down from my perch and stop crying. I do not want my son to slip away. I hold him as tight as I can. My son becomes my hope, casting a powerful light into my life. Without hesitation, like an ancient warrior who is gifted the skill of war, he fought demons and won. The *Shinigami* is gone. It takes no more than the unknown training of his early childhood years to face life's challenges with courage. Only the two of us live this moment. Only the two of us are judged. Only we know our family has been spared.

As my breathing steadies, I ask myself, *How did my ten-year-old son have the revelatory insight to come out to the garage at this exact moment to stop me?*

I nod my head, acknowledging that, at the age of ten, a part of him has been lost. His childhood innocence and freedom are gone forever. As we exit the garage, he solemnly accepts his predetermined role. That evening, a mystical bond and burden are forged, defining our purpose with great clarity. Richard heard and answered my silent pleas for help and, in doing so, became my mystical child.

2

Abandoned at Age Three

The immense pain I experience during that mystical 1962 moment starts at an early age. My recollection is that it originates in the summer of 1925, when I am a feisty three-year-old farm girl living in Pomona, California. Mom, with no explanation, dresses me in brand-new, blue apron pants. Could I be going visiting for the first time in my life? Yes. I am so thrilled, I can hardly contain myself.

Daddy packs my older sisters and me into our beat-up car. Off we go. The squeaky doors and crank-down windows make the trip noisy and exciting. Gusts of wind blow through the car as we rumble down the road. We pass a road sign welcoming us to Gardena. Shortly thereafter, we arrive at my auntie and uncle's farm, where a bright-red wagon greets us. My sisters take turns pulling me around the dusty yard. The dilapidated farmhouse, with its deep-brown outline, is marred by chipped siding, two broken windows, and a front door that creaks like a screaming ghost. I turn my back to it and pretend it is not there. My attention focuses on having fun playing with the red wagon.

Growing tired of pushing the wagon by myself, I notice that I am the only one laughing. I lift my head and scan the yard for Daddy and my sisters; they are gone. I run toward the front of the house, where Daddy parked our beat-up car. It is gone.

Puzzled and scared, I run to Auntie and ask, "Where's Daddy?"

Auntie kneels and takes my hand into hers. In a firm tone she says, "Tome, this is your new home, and you are to be our little girl."

I tremble and pull my hand away. "No!" I cry. "No. My daddy will come back for me. Daddy would never leave me."

Auntie folds her arms, towering over me, and repeats, "It has been decided; you are to be our little girl."

"Daddy accidentally forgot me!" I cry out.

As Auntie reaches out to me, I pull my hands to my side and run toward the dirt road leading away from the farm. I continue running as dirt flies behind me in a whirlwind of choking dust. I mutter, "Daddy accidentally forgot me."

When I reach the roadside, I look both ways for our car. I stand there and wait. When I get tired of standing in the blistering heat, I sit hugging my knees. I mull over what has happened, questioning and wondering. *What did I do wrong that Daddy would leave me?* I bite my parched lips to avoid crying, hoping to see the familiar, old, beat-up family car returning for me. The sun disappears below the distant horizon, and the day grows dark. My salty tears leave thin tracks on my face that feel scratchy to the touch.

My auntie quietly walks up to me, wets her fingers, and then wipes the evidence of my afternoon turmoil from my face. She extends her hand. I reluctantly accept it and walk back with her to the brightly lit farmhouse.

The next day I continue to maintain that Daddy accidentally forgot me and will return for me. I stoically stand by the roadside again, and then again the next day. As darkness descends, I know in my sad heart he is not coming for me. I defiantly march back to the little farmhouse and announce that from this day forward I will call my auntie and uncle "Mother" and "Father."

As my new life unfolds, I discover Mother is a stern taskmaster. She is hardworking, decisive, and strong-willed. Father is a kind, scholarly gentleman who is a lot of fun. His dark, bushy mustache reflects grayish highlights in the morning sunlight. Long hours in the harsh Southern California sun have chiseled deep-set wrinkles in his distinguished and honest face. His smile is simple and rarely missing. His short stature hides his strength. He often flips me onto his shoulders with ease. I follow him like a shadow. When he is getting ready to drive into town to fill up the faded-black Ford truck with gas or to buy hay for the horses, I happily take his old straw work hat into the house and run gaily back with his going-into-town hat tilted at an angle on my head.

I giggle and sing made-up songs to made-up tunes all the way into town and all the way back home.

When the Japanese musical and dancing troupes visit the local theater, Father loads us into the truck, and off we go to see

Tome with going-into-town hat

them. The music's cadence drums a comfortable heartbeat while the heat of the day withers away as the night matures. When we return home, I beg Mother and Father to sing the songs we just heard. They always frown at my request, but then they laugh and give in to my wishes. I love these nights and want more.

"Tome, let these nights be special," Mother says. "Too many will ruin the joy we get from them."

Father laughs and agrees. "Let them be special so you will cherish them."

Many nights after supper, we walk to visit neighbors. Father always carries me aloft on his big shoulders. He tells me, "I put you on my shoulders so you can get closer to the evening stars." When the night is clear I grab for those stars, hoping to capture one and take it home.

I learn that Father is a sociable man with many friends. Our house rings with laughter and happy voices. Although the exterior of our farmhouse is very dark, the inside is always brightly lit with the smiling faces of close friends. Neighbors know Mother is a better farmer than Father, but

Foster Father Tsuchiyama

he is a better master of ceremonies at parties and weddings. He is often called upon to help patch things up with feuding neighbors. These early days in my new home are filled with wonderful, soft hugs from Father, the smell of fresh wildflowers in our fields, and quiet nights occasionally interrupted by an old owl or the cry of coyotes or injured animals in the distance.

*   *   *

In the spring, the weather stays dark for weeks. Thick, gray rain clouds cluster tightly together, not allowing sunshine to break through. These gloomy days usher in my sixth birthday and Father's escalating complaints about stomach pains.

His doctor visits become more frequent, until one day Mother sits me down and says, "Tome, Father is extremely sick and requires an operation. He has something called cancer. We will need to be strong while he is away." Her typically piercing gaze softens, exposing her fear.

I run to Father and hug him as tightly as I can. Looking up at him, I declare, "Father, everything will be all right."

His mustache flips up, creating a warm smile, as he picks me up and whispers, "I will never leave you, Tome."

A few days later, a new blue car owned by our closest neighbor arrives to pick up Father and take him to the hospital. Our neighbors get out of the car, smile at me, and then help Father into their car. During one of Father's prior visits to see the doctor, he bought me a toy—a metal butterfly that flapped its wings as I pushed it along the ground—that I treasured and played with constantly. I loved it so much that when a wing fell off, I could not be consoled. On Father's last trip to the doctors, he bought me another one. After they depart for the hospital, I play all morning with my toy butterfly, my special gift from Father.

Early that evening, neighbors knock on our new screen door. No words are exchanged, only the side-to-side shaking of heads. Mother thanks them.

After they leave, Mother says, "Off to bed, Tome."

Walking down the hallway, I see Father's going-into-town hat hanging on a door hook. I wonder why he has not taken it with him. I see myself flipping it onto my head tomorrow, taking it with me to visit him.

Eager to visit Father, I rise early the next morning. Mother comes into my room and takes my hands into hers. Clumsily she says, "We will not be able to visit Father today," and walks away from me.

I reassure myself that everything is all right and he just needs more sleep. After several days pass, I ask Mother when we can visit Father. No answer.

Sunday morning comes and Mother helps me dress in my best outfit. Finally, I will be able to visit Father. I grab his going-into-town hat, knowing he will want it, and place it at a slight tilt onto my head. We drive through light rain in silence. We drive past the hospital and pull into the church parking lot. As we exit our truck, tears drip down Mother's cheeks and mix with the persistent raindrops.

Mother looks at me and chokes out, "This will be our last visit to see Father." Then she is silent for a long time.

Feeling betrayed, I lash out, "Mother, where is Father? Why are we here? Is the church taking care of him?"

Gathered around us are our neighbors, mostly Japanese farmers and white merchants. Mother and I are led to the front row of the church. At the base of the altar is an open casket. There, pale and silent, lies Father, arms crossed and eyes closed.

He promised me. He promised he would not leave me. I run up to the open casket and pound my fists on its metallic shell, screaming, "You promised.... You promised you would not leave me. I believed you."

As I fall to my knees, Mother quietly walks up to me. She helps me stand and slowly ushers me back to my seat.

Across every row of the church, tears fall. A woman I do not know comes up to me and holds my hand. Hunched over, she gifts me these words: "Tome, your father loved you with all his heart. There was not a moment he did not think about you or talk about you."

I look up to see a wrinkled woman with pale-brown eyes, smiling through her tears. "He will always love you, Tome. He will always be with you."

I turn my head to catch a glimpse of someone closing Father's casket. I drop my face into my hands, and his going-into-town hat falls off my head. I will never wear that hat again.

* * *

The next day I am up at five o'clock.

"Tome," Mother says, "our retired neighbors, the Weises, will come over and take care of you during the day while I am working."

I nod my head. I understand it is just the two of us now.

Distinguished Father Kawakita

This routine continues for three weeks. During this time, we receive a constant flow of friends. Without Father, I no longer feel the joy of their presence. A new face, bringing flowers, begins to visit us on a regular basis. I overhear Mother's friends say, "He is strong, honest, and from a very distinguished military family." They whisper, "He is Kawakita, a samurai family." He has a rumpled appearance, and he is neither sociable nor interested in the theater or cultural arts.

One Sunday morning, after he has been visiting for two months, twenty of our close friends bring food and gifts to our house. Mother helps me dress in my Sunday clothes. The last person to arrive is a distinguished-looking gentleman. His presence silences the crowd.

Mother bends down in front of me and says, "Tome, we will no longer be alone. I am marrying Kawakita-san." The distinguished gentleman turns to face me and smiles—it is Kawakita-san.

After the wedding ceremony, Kawakita-san drops to his knees and places his hand on my shoulder. He says, "I promise to never leave you."

I smile, hug him, and whisper, "Thank you, Father," but I do not believe him. I will be respectful and call him Father Kawakita. But someday, he will leave me, and I will not allow him to break my heart.

3

I Am the All-American Girl

In the spring of 1934, six years after Mother marries Father Kawakita, I mark my twelfth birthday. I am now one of the fastest and most athletic girls in school. Barely clearing five feet tall, I have slender, sturdy legs that support my agile body. My physique, my strength, and my endurance come from working on our farm. I am proud to be and want to be the epitome of the all-American farmer's daughter.

While Father Kawakita and Mother are in town picking up tools to repair our farm equipment, someone knocks on our front door. I move slowly to the door, open it a crack, and see that it is the retired German couple who live five acres away. Because my foster parents are always working outside or running into town for business, our neighbors, Mr. and Mrs. Weise, come over to check on me. Today, their wrinkled foreheads worry me.

"Hi, Tome," Mr. Weise says. "We've been discussing the dilemma with your given name, Tome. It's difficult to pronounce and sounds too masculine. It's just not fitting for an American girl."

An American girl. I like the sound of that.

Mr. Weise continues, "We tossed around several names amongst ourselves, but we want to hear your thoughts."

I get to choose my American name. I love it. After tossing names back and forth, we agree on Mary. Yes, Mary will be my new name. The Weises leave that afternoon feeling incredibly happy, knowing they helped me find my American name. I sit, smitten with it; my name is Mary. Now, I really feel like the all-American girl. From now on, I am Mary at school, with friends, with everyone.

Yet, even with my American name, Father Kawakita wants me to learn the Japanese tradition of the tea ceremony. He says, "Tome, it is important that you learn Japanese tea ceremony. It will help your mind to focus, gain discipline, and find tranquility." He doesn't razz me, but he mentions it several times, saying, "Even samurai learn tea ceremony."

I politely decline, due to my busy school and athletic schedule as well as my daily chores. My response is always, "I am an American farmer's daughter. Do I really need to learn Japanese traditions? Father Kawakita, I feel like I am being pulled in two different directions. I want to be the all-American farm girl. That's who I want to be." For weeks, I ignore his request and quietly retreat whenever it comes up in the conversation. It is not until a few months later that I give in.

In contrast to my all-American farmer's daughter image, Father Kawakita is not a farmer. He is a warrior, a thinker, and educated. His English is good, and his reasoning skills are beyond my understanding. He often uses his abacus to solve complex mathematical problems. His physical presence demands respect. I constantly hear people whisper,

"He is samurai." Although he does not smile as much as my former father, occasionally he laughs, and then immediately he looks straight through me with a stoic set of eyes. They are not angry or happy, just piercing and devoid of emotions.

I am fascinated by Father Kawakita's tales of mental and physical training. His stories suggest expecting the worst, knowing danger, preparing for it, and always being alert. His calm demeanor exemplifies his presence, reinforcing the power of his stories.

"I trained in the martial art of *jujutsu*, fighting unarmed, and *kenjutsu*, fighting with a katana," he told me. "I trained to anticipate, *sakki*, and not rely on my reactions alone. When training to fight, I faced multiple attackers. Responding to each attacker in isolation may mean a sudden defeat. It is only by simultaneously anticipating and countering each attacker's assault that I can be victorious. Again, victory will only come if I train my reflexes and mind to anticipate the worst and not be afraid of it. This training enables my mind to be pure and focused in the moment."

Mother is a farmer. But the farming cycle creates prolonged periods of spending with no income, and Father Kawakita expresses his concern that farming exposes our family to potential economic ruin. He wants a more stable stream of income. Although their perspectives differ, they reach a consensus over many dinner conversations. I listen to them talking and learn from Father Kawakita the importance of planning ahead for personal survival.

Standing outside our front door, I see the results of their conversations. Three thousand chickens now clutter our yard, roost and lay eggs in the coops, poop everywhere, and need constant protection from wild animals. We no longer grow crops to sell at harvest. We grow crops to feed our hungry chickens.

Each day I realize I am their slave. After I come home from school, I start the stove fire. Mother taught me how to start it and adjust the vents to keep it burning properly, and the importance of kindling and the proper type of wood. On this stove we set the big pots in which we heat wet rags used to clean the eggs Father Kawakita gathers from the nests. After they are cleaned, Mother places them on a scale and sorts them by weight into different wooden boxes. Each day we sell our eggs, and each day we receive cash or barter.

In the summer of 1934, when school is not in session, I work six days a week. This includes wheeling loads of manure into outdoor bins and using a hoe to scrape out the chicken coops. I develop painful blisters on my hands from pushing the heavy wheelbarrow. I also clean the poultry water containers near the coops, where our geese guard the chickens and chase me around. I run for my life from the squawking male birds pecking at my legs, defending myself with a bucket. Yes, I am a slave to these chickens.

While working outdoors, more than in any previous year, I am approached by many emaciated, older white farmers with gaunt faces, asking if we need help and if we can pay them for their work. I am cautious, scared, and hesitant to talk with them, until two farm boys who look about my age ask for work. They are walking scarecrows. Father Kawakita emerges from the field to make sure I am okay.

"How old are you boys and where are you from?" he asks.

One boy says, "I am from Oklahoma."

The other boy says, "I am from Missouri."

They both answer, "We're eighteen."

Why are they flooding into California and looking for work? I see they are like us, farmers trying to survive.

"We have no work to offer you," Father Kawakita says softly.

As they walk away, their silhouettes cast a shadow of starvation. Their departure haunts me. I appreciate Father Kawakita's insight in transforming our livelihood from farming to raising chickens. He anticipated these times and saved us.

*   *   *

In the fall of 1934, I advance another grade. Running after a basketball while playing in the Girls Athletic Association (GAA) on a cool afternoon, I trip and fall. When I get up, my legs feel wobbly. I think nothing of it, just another scraped knee. The next day at school, as I am dribbling a basketball, my feet get in the way and I trip and fall again. Disgusted with my uncoordinated running, I sit for a moment, upset with myself. This time, getting to my feet is difficult—my muscles do not cooperate.

After school, when I am doing my chores around the farm, I complain to Mother, "I am having trouble walking. My muscles hurt and I am so tired." She dismisses my complaints, then ignores me.

The next day at school, I fall again. As I get up, my legs wobble uncontrollably and I fall again. I am sent home by the school nurse with my knees bleeding and bandaged.

One of my teachers volunteers to take me home. She drops me off on the road that runs past the edge of our farm. The bright sunlight makes it difficult to get a clear view of the house. Blinded by the light, I place my left hand on my forehead to shade against the glare. My sole thought is to lie down and rest my trembling body, beaten by fatigue. I take one measured step, but my second step sends me stumbling across the driveway, where I fall face-first onto the lumpy dirt. The grit grinds into my hands and face. I see small droplets of blood oozing from my palms, and I feel a stinging sensation where my face hit the dirt driveway. I swipe my right hand across my cheeks to try and brush off the debris, but that only smears dirt over them. Now, muddy brown tears are streaming down my face. The pain in my muscles grips me like a vise, making me helpless.

From deep inside me comes a high-pitched scream. "Help me!"

I hear Mother yell out "I'm coming" followed by a distant *thud*. She must have dropped whatever she was carrying at the time.

I gasp with relief, "Thank you."

When she reaches me, she tries to pick me up but is unable to lift me. Her squinched face projects frustration, and she screams for help. Mother now knows I am not playing a game. I truly cannot walk.

Again, Mother cries out for help. In the distance I see the faint image of someone running toward us. When the face comes into focus, I recognize Father Kawakita. Although his demeanor is calm, as usual, he is bearing down on us and does not stop. With one smooth motion he picks me up from the ground and commands Mother to get the truck keys.

Mother runs into the house and quickly reemerges with the keys, the screen door slamming behind her. She quickly opens the door of our family truck, and Father Kawakita gently places me in the center of the bench seat and then lunges onto the driver's side. Mother, sitting on the passenger side, frantically rocks and cradles me. Father Kawakita turns the key in the ignition, which creates a terrible grinding sound. The truck does not start. He calmly turns the key again. More grinding sounds follow. Mother continues rocking me while her feet and hands fidget. Finally, the rumble of the engine fills my ears. Father Kawakita pulls on the floor-mounted gear shifter and launches us down the dusty road toward town.

Later that afternoon, the doctor examines me, periodically grunting "*umm.*" After his final test, he leaves me and joins Mother and Father Kawakita in the adjacent room. Sitting alone in his yellowing examination room, I detect low whispers coming from the three of them. When the whispering stops, I hear footsteps and then Mother pops her head in the doorway. She takes one step forward and stands there, straight and tall, staring at me. One tear, trickling down her cheek, turns into several. She takes a few more slow steps forward and sits down beside me. She reaches over and holds my hand for longer than I could ever remember. We are silent, but I feel her deep warmth and caring. At that moment, she is not Mother—she is my mom.

Father Kawakita comes in, expressionless and emotionless, picks me up, and carries me to our truck. No words are spoken. The bumpy ride rocks me like a cradle. I drift between sleep and groggy awareness. When we arrive home, Mother excuses me from my afternoon chores and Father Kawakita suggests I rest. I lie in bed, wondering what has happened and what is wrong with me.

At dinnertime, Father Kawakita comes into my room, hoists me up, and carries me to the dinner table. The three of us sit and eat in complete silence. After dinner, Mother clears the table, this being my normal chore. She sits back down and looks at Father Kawakita and then directly at me. The eerie silence is broken by Mother's long, drawn-out breath, but she does not speak. She only begins to cry, looking down through tear-soaked eyes.

Father Kawakita places his hand on my shoulder and sighs. His eyes are sad, and his eyebrows are lowered into a deep frown. Slowly and deliberately, he whispers, "Tome, you have polio."

4

Crippled by Life

In the spring of 1934, I was one of the fastest girls in school. In the fall of 1934, I am sentenced to be a cripple. After Father Kawakita tells me I have polio, I am too stunned to cry. I look down so that Father Kawakita and Mother do not see my fear. My limbs are no longer a part of me. Back in bed, I wonder what life will be like, unable to run, possibly unable to walk or, someday, unable to breathe on my own. I immediately take a deep breath. Could this really be happening to me?

Coming back to school after being diagnosed with polio proves challenging. My weak legs and ankles still fit well within my neatly pulled-up and folded bobby socks, but they lack coordination. Luckily, I can still wear my favorite brown-and-white saddle shoes. It is emotionally painful sitting in class, hiding my emaciated legs. When GAA time comes, I sit on the sideline, my anger growing. *Why did God give me this handicap?*

"Mary, when will you be able to run with us again? We need you," exclaims Eloise Geisert. Eloise, whom we call

Gizzy, is a strong, dark-haired girlfriend who is always smiling. We share GAA, and I have always chosen her for my basketball team.

"Maybe never!" I scream back. "Can't you see my legs? . . . I am crippled."

Stunned, Gizzy walks away and onto the basketball court. I fume, questioning why she would ask such a dumb question. Can't she see I have polio? Can't she see I am a cripple? Stupid girl.

Then Gizzy turns around and walks toward me with a smile. Why is she smiling? I'm not smiling.

"Gizzy, go away!" I yell.

She drops her head and turns her back to me.

I look down at my legs and slam my fists against them, muttering, "I hate my pathetic legs."

*　*　*

Weeks go by and I hobble between classes. I hate everyone. I hate the stares and the giggling behind my back. I hate my teachers for treating me differently. I hate my classmates, especially when I watch them running. Consumed with self-hate and self-pity, I stop talking to people. Why did this happen to me? I hate God for doing this to me. It is not fair. My grades are falling, and I do not care. It just does not matter. Who will marry a cripple? Who will employ a cripple?

While I am sitting by myself in the corner of the outside lunch area, someone yells, "Mary, follow me." It is the commanding voice of the beautiful Lois Norman, with movie-star skin and wavy hair. She gives me a cold and glassy stare. "Mary, follow me."

Lois is a good friend from GAA whom I admire, as she is an honor student and we share a love for the theater and movies. Dutifully, I struggle to my feet. Lois begins walking away from me and toward a double-door entry on the side of the school's main brick building. Dragging one leg, I try to keep up. Lois does not look back but appears to gauge her steps so I will not fall too far behind. She enters the building, and I follow. When she reaches the door to the first classroom, she stops and turns around.

"Mary," she says in a softer voice, "I am tired of you feeling sorry for yourself."

She opens the classroom door. Just as I am about to scream at Lois that I do not care what she thinks and I can do whatever I want, a chorus of girls sings out, "Mary, we aren't going to feel sorry for you anymore."

There, in the classroom, are twenty of my GAA girlfriends, each holding a candle; they light up the room and temporarily blind me. The candlelight is reflected in the collective tears on their cheeks. Again, they sing out, "Mary, we aren't going to feel sorry for you anymore."

Facing my GAA girlfriends, my voice cracking under the weight of my emotions, I whisper, "I'm not going to feel sorry for me anymore."

This circle of friends engulfs me in a warmth that lifts my darkness. The power of their friendship provides a positive path forward. Later that afternoon, while lying on my bed at home, I fall asleep envisioning the day when I can run in the fields again.

When I open my eyes after a short nap, I find a dozen short ropes lying across my bed. To keep me occupied, Father Kawakita is teaching me how to tie different knots, a skill he learned while working on fishing and exploration boats and making nooses to trap animals that invade our farm. He tells me there are patterns in knot tying, and learning to tie knots will help me see other patterns in life.

Days pass, and observing that my polio symptoms are not improving, the Weises come to visit in the evening so they can have a conversation with Mother and Father Kawakita. I am sent to my bedroom while the adults talk. I linger in the hallway and overhear the Weises suggesting a doctor who is familiar with the work of someone called Sister Kenny, who has successfully treated polio in Australia.

More importantly, Mr. Weise says, "Our doctor friend has researched and studied the origins of the polio virus and may know how to improve Mary's condition before it turns into a permanently crippling situation."

I lean around the corner to try and catch a glimpse of the Weises as they describe their doctor friend.

Mother scolds, "Mary?"

Mr. Weise quickly responds, "Tome." He appears embarrassed but continues to push the idea of a new doctor for me. His final words are "Our friend won't charge you, as she is a saint in all respects."

Two days later, Mother, Father Kawakita, and I visit the new doctor recommended by Mr. Weise. She is a kind Scottish English lady, Elmina Farquhar Cook, MD, who suggests I eat cooked vegetables, clean out my intestines with warm-water enemas, and drink a lot of clean, warm water. She stresses the importance of keeping my intestines clean and clear.

That night, after returning from our visit with Dr. Cook, Father Kawakita tucks me into bed and sits beside me.

"Tome," he says, "you must look beyond what you cannot see. To imagine beyond who you are, to grow beyond your present character marks the soul of a great person.... You can be that person. We may not see miracles coming at us or upon us. These times are difficult, but you must go beyond what at first appears impossible."

When I open my eyes, I am alone. The bright corners of my room and the farm are hidden by the shadows of night.

* * *

Three days turn into several months. Dr. Cook's suggested regimen leaves me thin and feeling much better. On one uniquely special Tuesday morning, December 25, 1934, after months of treatment and care, I slowly place my legs over the edge of my bed, and my feet meet the cold floor. I inhale the strength of a new morning and lift my torso. I stand upright and smile. Laboring less with each measured step, I confidently walk into the kitchen, where Father Kawakita and Mother are sitting to have breakfast. Stunned, Father Kawakita starts to get up to help me, but I wave at him to stop. I walk to the table, without a limp, and take my place.

Dr. Cook's Letter— curing Tome of Polio

Father Kawakita smiles and looks up toward the heavens. "Miracles do happen," he says, "when discipline, integrity of purpose, and courage come together. Tome, I am proud of you."

This is the best Christmas ever.

*   *   *

Three months later, in 1935, I celebrate my thirteenth birthday. My gifts are the return of my leg strength, my emotional balance, and my competitive spirit. Reclaiming my status as one of the fastest girls in school, with polio behind me, I am thankful to be able to run and jump.

Today, I smile and remember that being happy is easy when you are healthy and surrounded by people who love you.

Shortly after my birthday in 1935, I meet a new girl in our school. She is from Idaho, a bit shy, and rumors circulate that she has a damaged heart. Her name is Mary Uyeda. We share each lunchtime and become best friends.

Being fiercely competitive and good at playing volleyball, basketball, and softball means I am given my first choice of teammates. I always pick the fastest and strongest girls. No one picks Mary Uyeda, and I see her ignoring us. I like her, but I want to win.

After school, while helping Father Kawakita clean eggs, I ask, "Father Kawakita, should I feel bad that I do not choose my best friend, Mary Uyeda, when we play sports at school? I just want to win and be the best."

Father Kawakita stops cleaning eggs and gently places them down on a wet cleaning cloth. His complete attention is on me. "Tome," he says, "what is winning? What is losing? Can there be honor in both? Does Mary Uyeda want to play? Do you feel an allegiance to her as a trusted friend? Do you have compassion for her disability? If you respect Mary and feel loyal to her, why don't you choose her for your team?"

I look down, ashamed of my earlier decisions. I have always wanted to pick Mary Uyeda—she is my best friend—but I don't want to lose.

"Tome, it is your decision. It is your life. It is your philosophy to live by."

"Humph." I walk away, mumbling, "Tomorrow..."

The next day, when choosing teams for basketball, I choose Mary Uyeda.

Timidly, she walks up to me. "Mary, why pick me? I am not as good as the other girls.... You may lose."

"Mary Uyeda, a winning team without my best friend is no winning team at all."

Mary Uyeda's smile radiates. Together we play to win. I now understand my conversation with Father Kawakita. I do not care that Mary Uyeda struggles due to the aftermath of rheumatic fever. I do not care that she laughs more than she scores points. I care that we are best friends. Her enlarged heart may have weakened her physically, but our friendship strengthens our team. No one else chooses Mary Uyeda except me. But I see her as the most valuable player, and we win many times.

Resuming my athletics at school increases my appetite and continues to improve my health. Mother's health and stress, though, are moving in the opposite direction.

One day before dinner, Mother drags herself into our house and comes to me. "Tome, last night on the radio,

Father and I heard about a book called *The Great Depression*, written by Lionel Robbins. It describes what is happening to all of us, why times have been so difficult. Have you discussed the Great Depression in school?"

Fidgeting, I say, "No, but many of my friends have mentioned that their parents constantly argue about money."

"Now that you are better," Mother says, "we expect you to start doing your chores again. We need your help."

"Really?" I whine.

"You are no longer sick. Being lazy at home will not be tolerated. We are lucky to have chickens and eggs to support us. They are our survival, so we must work hard and take good care of them."

This translates into working six days a week again.

One Saturday Mary Uyeda comes to visit, and Mother acknowledges my hard work by excusing me from my Saturday chores until after Mary Uyeda goes home. Mother allows us to listen to the radio in the living room. This is special, as listening to the radio is typically reserved for programs of a serious nature. We marvel at the radio announcer's story of Amelia Earhart's flight from Hawaii to California. We make a promise that we will do something great after we graduate high school. For now, I wish for Christmas to bring us the new Parker Brothers board game, Monopoly.

After Mary Uyeda goes home and I have completed my chores, I lie on my bed, wondering what my siblings are doing. There are eight of them, one brother and seven sisters. Mother once let it slip that I am the fifth of nine children. Until recently, I put my memories of them in a safe place, not to be visited. It hurts so much to imagine my parents giving me away and they all doing fine without me. Maybe I never existed to them. Maybe I should do the same. Many times, I ask, *Why was I the only child of nine to be given away? What did I do wrong?* It has been ten years since I saw them, and I cannot remember what they look like. I do not know where they live, and I do not know how to contact them.

After school sports today, Mary Uyeda asks, "Mary, why are you so sad?"

"I do not know. Sometimes I feel all alone. Sometimes I feel so very alone." For no apparent reason, I drop to my knees and begin crying.

Luckily, Mary Uyeda is here. "*Kawaisou* [kah-WAI-soh]," she mutters. In Japanese this means "pitiful or poor thing." Mary Uyeda's mood quickly shifts to comical. "Mary, you'll scare off the boys if you keep crying."

"What boys?" I pop up, trying to fix my hair, and look around.

Mary Uyeda starts to laugh, and I join her.

* * *

During my high school years in Gardena, my longtime GAA friends and Mary Uyeda continually perk me up and make this period of my life a delight. They are my close school siblings, my family. One Saturday each month, Mary Uyeda and I go to the movie theater. Today we are going to see the movie *Boys Town*, starring Spencer Tracy.

"Why do you like Spencer Tracy?" Mary Uyeda says. "He is no Cary Grant or Clark Gable. He is not even handsome."

"It's because he's real," I say. "He projects an inner strength and warmth. I just like him."

"Okay, but next month I would like to see Cary Grant in *Gunga Din*. Okay?"

"Absolutely."

I cherish these moments with Mary Uyeda. Between our lunchtime talks, playing sports, and watching movies, we build great memories.

After I return home from one of our movie Saturdays, Mother asks, "Tome, what do you love about high school?"

I frown, and then say, "I like my home economics class. Learning how to sew my own clothes and budget home finances has really helped me save money for advanced language school."

Mother smiles. "Good," she says.

"I love the arts, singing, dancing," I ramble on, "and acting in our school plays."

Mother frowns at this response. She begins scolding me and telling me these are foolish things. No matter, I will not change my answer.

Friends such as Lois Norman provide positive feedback about what I love in high school. After seeing me perform in a school play, she tells me I have an amazing singing voice. While this may attract the boys, it is Lois who is the picture of a Hollywood starlet. I envy her regal looks and perfect poise. This year she becomes our honor student representative to the Shakespearean Festival.

One night during my senior year, while washing dishes at home, I mention to Mother that I have been asked out on dates. Mother is extremely strict and keeps me close to home. She does not allow me to date. I have a crush on a young man, Kenny, who is destined to be a medical doctor. We smile at each other every day, but he never asks me out.

I even try to make him jealous by talking to his friends and ignoring him. Nothing works. As our senior year comes to an end, Kenny skips graduation. Instead, he packs to go overseas to attend a Japanese college, and then medical school. But I know our paths will cross in the future.

When Mother hears of Kenny's departure, she says, "Good boy, but not for you. I do not approve of him."

"Why don't you approve of Kenny?" I plead. "You are friends with his family."

"Going to Japan for school—what for? Waste of money," Mother mutters.

In June 1940, I graduate from Gardena High School. I continue working and living on the farm during the summer, but I plan to attend a two-year advanced language school starting in September. I have dreams of becoming an interpreter or teacher. From the fall of 1940 and through 1941, I commute by bus to Compton for school.

On Sunday mornings I usually attend church alongside other farm kids in Gardena. Today, December 7, 1941, is no exception. The afternoon is filled with small chores and studying for next week's school lessons. Our Sunday dinner is filled with our typical chitchat. Afterward, I am cleaning up in the kitchen before joining Mother and Father in the living room for our Sunday evening ritual of sitting around our radio, listening to Walter Winchell on the NBC Blue Network talk about world news. While I am hand-drying the last dish, Mother screams. I run into the living room to find her kneeling and sobbing. Father Kawakita is by her side, holding her as she rocks back and forth.

1940 Gardena High School yearbook: Mary (Tome) Nakashima, Lois Norman, Gizzy, and Mary Uyeda

"Father Kawakita, what's wrong? What can I do to help?"

Father Kawakita looks up. "The Japanese Imperial Navy attacked Pearl Harbor in Hawaii this morning. On Walter Winchell's *Jergen's Journal* broadcast tonight, he announced that the Department of Justice is looking to incarcerate all Japanese nationals as soon as possible. This includes immediately seizing their property. National security is now our first priority."

The remainder of the evening is a blur.

After a restless night's sleep, I awake the next morning, exhausted. I immediately get dressed to find out what is happening. Mother and Father Kawakita are outside working as if nothing has happened.

"Father Kawakita, is there more news?"

"Not yet. For now we focus on work. This evening we will listen to the radio. Until we know more, we focus on today. Worrying does not help."

I nod and skip school to help on the farm.

When evening comes, we sit around the radio. Walter Winchell announces, "Our president's declaration of war against Japan was presented to Congress today and approved in less than one hour. Today, we are officially at war with Japan."

When I am nineteen years old, my foster parents become enemies of the country. The days that follow bring pockets of hysteria and nightly blackouts that form a backdrop to a surreal landscape. Japanese farmers try to retreat and lock themselves away within the shelter of their homes. FBI agents, men in dark suits, knock on many doors and take Japanese fathers and grandfathers into custody. Fear spreads like wildfire. Unlike many other Japanese American families, I feel safe, for I know Father Kawakita will protect us.

5

The Hysteria of War

Confusion, posted signs saying NO JAPS, broken windows, and people screaming obscenities fill what was once a serene landscape. We live in a community of hardworking Japanese farmers and white merchants who shake hands on their deals and follow through on their promises. The weak and ugly side of humanity rears its head, and I am troubled by its features.

On a gray, overcast April day in 1942, I take the bus to visit Mary Uyeda. Her parents' farmhouse is nothing more than a bungalow with an attached front porch. I knock on Mary's front door, on which there is taped an official-looking poster that reads INSTRUCTIONS TO ALL PERSONS OF JAPANESE ANCESTRY.

I read the poster heading, but the small print below is too much work to decipher, so I ignore it. I walk around the house and peer into the first window, which has been shattered. I walk around to the back of the house. All the windows are shattered. I look into the house and see large bricks lying on the empty floors. Why did Mary move and not tell me? I am her best friend. Dejected, I slowly walk the long road home.

A ball of dust soon envelops me, and the sound of rolling car tires precedes the appearance of a convertible full of high school friends. They stop to chat.

"Did you hear?" Plumia Leach, a basketball teammate with wavy hair and perfect makeup, gasps. "They took Kenny's dad away in a big black car. Why are they taking our friends' parents?"

"Mary," she continues, "you should go home to comfort your mom. I know she is friends with Kenny's dad. Are your parents at risk? You are one of my oldest best friends—are you at risk? Oh, Mary, I am so sorry for all this." The concern on Plumia's face is sincere, as her love for cosmetic perfection would not allow her to wrinkle her forehead so much otherwise.

I reach over to hug her. "Thank you, Plumia . . . ."

As I step away from our hug, Plumia asks, "Do you want a ride home?"

"Maybe not. I want to walk," I say quickly.

I wave goodbye as her dark-reddish hair fans the coming sunset. She and the others speed off down the road toward town. It is getting dark. I could catch a bus but walking suits me as I am mad at Mary Uyeda for leaving without saying goodbye. During my walk I ask myself, *Am I at risk? I am an American citizen, the all-American farm girl. How could I be at risk?*

When I reach home, Mother and Father Kawakita are packing. Boxes, taped shut and marked FRAGILE, are all around me.

"Why are we packing things?" I ask politely.

Mother, looking angry, ignores my question.

Father Kawakita calmly whispers, "It's war, and we must preserve what we need and what we cherish. The people buying the chicken farm have promised to keep our things safe for us. They have allowed us to store things in the cellar." He continues his trek, carrying boxes to the cellar.

Mother scowls and curses. "They will not honor that.... They have bought our life's work for a pittance. They are no better than smiling thieves."

Searching for a friendly face, I ask, "Where's Suzy?"

Suzy is our German shepherd. Mother wanted a watchdog, and when I was alone and fighting polio, Suzy gained my trust as a faithful companion.

Father Kawakita has returned from the cellar and hears my question. "We have given her to our neighbors, the Weises. She will have a good home with them." Mother does not look up but continues to busily pack, ignoring me.

At first, I am angry, then saddened, about losing our dog. *Why are we giving away our dog, and why are we selling things so cheap? What is going on?* First my best friend abandons me, and now my foster parents are running away. I do not understand.

Father Kawakita stops packing our Japanese woodblock prints and mumbles, "It has become dangerous for us to stay." He points to the kitchen table. "Tome, please sign these papers."

Father Kawakita never runs from tough times. *Why are Mother and Father Kawakita shattering my life?* This is unheard of from him. He taught me to face my fears and go forward, even if I think it is impossible. We are not leaving. This is my home.

"I will not abandon the place where I feel safe," I whimper. "I will not sign these papers."

Mother runs away, crying. Father Kawakita reaches out, places his hand on my shoulder, and sits me down. This soothes my frayed nerves.

"Tome, I must think of the safety of our family." Father Kawakita's furry eyebrows are drawn together, and the words seem to be squeezed from his lips. "We are no longer safe here. We have too many Japanese friends, and your mother and I are not citizens and can never become citizens because of the law and because we are not white." His voice is unwavering.

I pick up the pen. I read the papers on the kitchen table. I flip to the last page and sign it. We no longer have a home.

6

Me Facing Me

One week has passed since the day I signed away our home. Today is a cloud-covered April morning in 1942. Mother and Father Kawakita are waiting for me at the front door.

Mother is formally dressed, as if for a visit to friends on any holiday Sunday. Upon seeing me, she says, "Tome, we need to get to the trains on time, no dilly-dallying this morning." Return of the taskmaster. Her strict demeanor is comforting.

She places a numbered tag in my palm and slowly folds my hand around it. "Do not lose this tag." The string from the tag dangles between my fingers. I quickly attach it to my suitcase handle. Twenty years of life belongings now fit neatly into it.

Mother and Father Kawakita have kept our move a secret, and I have been too busy with my advanced language school to take notice of anything else. I hope our destination is by the ocean, or an exotic countryside where we may farm and raise chickens among hills of tall, waving grass. I picture traveling across the country by train to someplace sunny, where there is always a cool breeze tossing my hair.

A knock on our front door breaks into my daydream, and I hear the deep voice of Mr. Weise. Looking somber, he says, "We are deeply troubled to see you go."

Mother and Father Kawakita silently nod their heads in agreement.

"Mary, let me help you with your suitcase."

Mother looks up, scoffs.

"Mary, let me help you with your suitcase," Mr. Weise repeats.

He is such a gentleman. I thank him as he lifts my suitcase and then opens the car door for me. Stepping into his new car makes me feel special. Mother and I sit in the back seat while Father Kawakita and Mr. Weise sit in the front, talking in hushed tones, their conversation muffled. The ride to the train station gives me time to say goodbye to the familiar open fields and parts of the city I have been allowed to explore. Cool air skims along the partially open window, encouraging my eyes to close and drying my tears.

Upon arriving at the train station, I look over to Mother and ask, "Is it too late to go back home?" She ignores my comment and maintains her silence.

When the car stops, I open the car door and step out onto the sidewalk. After Mother, Father Kawakita, and Mr. Weise exit, we all walk to the back of the car and pull our suitcases and filled pillowcases from the trunk. With our life belongings by our side, Mother, Father Kawakita, and I bow to Mr. Weise. He acknowledges our thank-you with a nod, and he then gets in his car and drives away. No words spoken. We brush ourselves off and walk toward the train station.

We step inside and start our trek to the platform. I am dazzled by the décor. This wonderment doesn't last long, as I am quickly overtaken by the smell of burning oil and possibly coal steam. Dizziness blurs my vision, taking me back to when I was three years old, waiting for my father to come back for me. Like then, no one is coming to save me. I walk in a trance, blinded by the daylight.

I nearly stumble into uniformed soldiers carrying guns and ordering people around. Ahead of me, I watch Japanese grandmothers and Japanese grandfathers form narrow lines into each train car. No one is crying, but a solemn, indignant air lingers. I turn to my left. In front of me are large, open train windows. I can see people inside. No one looks back at me. They all bow their heads, as if they are projecting a great shame. I suddenly stop, my trance ended.

Why am I here? Why are there so many armed soldiers? Why is there such shame in the air? I feel this is all wrong. The setting, the people, the circumstances are all wrong. *Sakki*, a spiritual aspect of Bushido that anticipates an attack before it physically manifests, overcomes me. I am in danger. It is imminent.

Behind me a soldier yells, "Jap girl, get a move on—you're holding us up."

Who is he yelling at? I look around and am confronted by another large soldier with a rifle butt in hand who grimaces when he sees my face.

In a threatening tone, he shouts, "Get moving, Jap girl. Where's your number? Where's your number tag? Why aren't you wearing your number tag?"

Wearing it? I look away. I thought the number tag Mother gave me was for my suitcase. How could it be for me?

Pointing to my suitcase, I scream at the soldier, "This is my number tag, on my suitcase. My name is Mary. I am not a number. I am a person. I am the all-American girl at the Saturday matinee movies. I am an athlete, a dancer, a singer. I am Mary."

"Jap girl, who the hell do you think you are?" the soldier yells again. "Don't you get it? You're just a number. Keep moving."

I turn back to him and yell, "My name is Mary, and I am no Jap girl. I was born here. I grew up here. I am an American citizen."

I am not afraid. *Sakki*, I sense the danger, but I will fight for who I am.

The soldier angrily steps forward. He is so close, I can feel his breath on my forehead. Mother wedges her way in between the soldier and me. She grabs my arm, yanks me through the nearest train door, and forces me down onto the seat. Her eyes are focused only on me.

"Tome," Mother says, "today you are a Jap girl."

I look around the train car but can see no one acknowledging this moment. Everyone is silent.

"I am Mary, not some Jap girl," I scream, angry and confused. "I am not your real daughter, and I am—"

Mother raises her right hand and, with a swift sideways motion, slaps my face. My hair clip and dribble from my mouth fly across the train car. My face burns hot. Mother raises her right hand again, signaling that silence is demanded. Through my tears, I look out the open train window and see the soldiers outside the train, laughing and dismissing me as if I were a spoiled child. I see Father Kawakita running with my suitcase, tossing it into another train car just before he jumps onto the train.

A violent jerk of the train throws me onto the floor. As it pulls away from the station, engine smoke spews across white people on the platform who are waving goodbye. Lois and Plumia are frantically jumping up and down, trying to catch my attention. I do not want to acknowledge them, not now. Refocusing my gaze, I try to look out the train window on the opposite side. It's closed, and this time, I see the reflection of a young Jap girl, crying. My reflection in the train window shatters my constructed reality and exposes the truth.

Today, I am no longer the all-American girl. Today, I surrender to the truth spoken by Mother and confirmed by the soldiers. Reflected in that train window is me, a visual immigrant in the eyes of America. Resigned, I fall in line with the other passengers and bow my head in shame. I am Mary Tome Nakashima, and I am ashamed and afraid of being a Jap girl. This is the danger that I face.

Part Two

Prison, Poverty, and Prejudice

I am a citizen of the United States of America. I am not accused or convicted of a crime. Due to my Japanese heritage, and only that, I am incarcerated at the age of twenty, without due process. My face, my physical presence, doom me to be treated as an enemy of the country I love. The chapters in Part Two capture life behind barbed wire and surrounded by armed guard towers, where I become a wife and a mother, and my subsequent release from my prison in the Gila River Camp, and the war I fight against poverty, racism, and self-doubt. This period marks the beginning of understanding my *ikigai*, and how I will gift it to my son, Richard.

7

Shame, Guilt, and Courage

We are told to close all the windows. The landscape flying by is hidden behind blackout shades—the first lost freedom is not being allowed to see the world around me. I reflect on my startling encounter with the soldiers. How naïve and sheltered I have been. I believed I was an equal. I believed I was the same as Lois and Gizzy. I know I look different, but so do Lois and Plumia. Both the soldiers and Mother called me a Jap girl. Why did I not see this before? I did not know I was looked down upon as inferior. I did not know I was just a number. Pondering all of this makes the five-hour ride heading northeast noticeably short. I wonder what other freedoms I will lose next.

Disrupting my thoughts, Mother says, "Tulare is a city in the Central Valley of California. It will be our new home for a few months."

The train abruptly stops. Soldiers begin walking through the train cars, shouting, "Collect your suitcases and other belongings from the baggage train car. We are getting off here. After you find your belongings, form a single line, stay close together, and follow us a short distance through town, where buses will then take us to the fairgrounds. We are your escorts."

Exiting the train, my legs are wobbly, and my body aches from the bumpy train ride. I hobble down the train-car stairs and step to the left. Mother, Father Kawakita, and I make our way to the baggage car and, working together, pull down our belongings. We clutch what is left of our lives. I look around but don't see a train station. We are in the middle of town.

I glance forward and watch a thin line of hunched-over passengers snaking their way into formation. Led and flanked by soldiers holding rifles with bayonets attached, we begin our walk through town.

Encumbered by a heavy suitcase, my pace slows, reflecting my physical fatigue. Occasionally, I glance to the right, then to the left. Locals are scowling at us and mouthing obscenities. The faint sounds of the words "damn Japs" pierce the air many times. Shivers run down my neck and back. I succumb to the cold, menacing stares of hatred with my fear wedged between my sniffles and tears. Father Kawakita was right; we are not safe.

After boarding the bus, I sit down and see block-like structures in the distance. They come into focus as we edge closer. The fairground ahead welcomes us with the stench of livestock shit. This inviting aroma is produced by the recently mucked-out horse stalls that are my new home. A hissing sound as the bus slows announces our arrival. I step off the bus and grab my belongings.

The stench intensifies, burning my eyes and overwhelming my senses. I take a few short steps and my gut spasms. I stop walking and hunch over as my stomach contracts violently. My eyes begin watering copiously. With one big retching sound I lurch forward and throw up a brown-and-red mixture. My vomit splatters on the loose dirt in front of me and covers my shoes. I breathe in slowly, hoping I don't feel the urge again. People behind me begin walking around me and my mess. Not acknowledging them, I continue marching forward and join the registration line. The nauseous rawness in my throat lingers, and I fidget as we wait our turn.

Mother taps me and says, "Tome, we must all have the same last name, or they will separate us. Father has adopted you so we can stay together. You are now Mary Tome Kawakita. You are officially his daughter and a member of his family."

I am an American citizen. My name is Nakashima. Why must I change my name? We are family. They wouldn't separate us over our last name.

"Jap girl, what's your name?" The white administrator's voice startles me.

I look at Mother, then down at the ground, and mutter, "Tome Kawakita. My American name is Mary." Then I ask sarcastically, "What does it mean to be an American citizen? Is it different for people who look different? Is my life worth anything?"

Without looking up, the administrator grunts, "Next."

After the initial sting of having to change my name wears off, I cautiously explore the campgrounds. I find the mess hall, the latrines, and the infirmary. The more I discover about our camp of five thousand, cast into a California wasteland between Fresno and Bakersfield, the more I am in awe.

Over the next several weeks, I witness the emergence of normal, day-to-day activities. A collection of disciplined routines and traditions forms a settling aura that helps the camp dwellers cope with their abrupt displacement. The adaptability of these Japanese Americans makes me proud to be one. Father Kawakita is wrong; surrounded by our many Japanese friends, by people who look like me, I feel safer.

There are problems.

I hate the horrible sanitary conditions. The latrines have no partitions, and there is no privacy. We devise make-shift solutions: using cardboard or having friends hold up a sheet. What's worse, the water pressure is so low that even the flushing toilets are filthy with built-up excrement, which smells rancid and attracts flies. My perpetual diarrhea is a constant reminder of the terrible sanitation, the indigest-ible food, the cramped quarters, and the excruciating heat. Another freedom is lost.

* * *

During the first three months, I vacillate between depres-sion, anxiety, and hope. Today, as I did yesterday, I ask myself, *Why am I an inmate at twenty years old when I did nothing wrong?*

Mother retreats into a mental shell, and Father Kawakita, while present, is very quiet. Without their help, I am alone. I want to go home. I want the comfort of my bed, not the stiff canvas army cot issued to me. I want the security of our land and our neighbors. I want the familiar weather, and I want the freedom to venture where and when I choose.

The barbed-wire fences surrounding the camp and the armed soldiers along the perimeter are not here to protect us. They are here to ensure we are obedient. My naïveté is shattered, replaced by the knowledge that this is not a camp, this is not an assembly center—this is a prison. I have lost all my freedoms.

During the fourth month, each new day decomposes what's alive inside me. There is no normal in my life. My hopefulness while the situation was still new is gone. A hot, steamy August day in 1942 finds me standing outside our makeshift residence, screaming at the sky. Then, exhausted, I walk into our horse-stall home to find Mother and Father Kawakita repacking our meager belongings, preparing us for travel.

"Tome, we are moving to the Gila River Camp in Arizona," Father Kawakita quickly volunteers. "It is extremely hot there, and we will need to be vigilant to avoid scorpions and large insects. During the winters it will be bitter cold."

I envision a small cottage with cool, running water and a proper outhouse with walls. These thoughts are refreshing, but delusional, and our horse stall of a home reminds me that I am still a prisoner, held against my will.

This time when the soldiers order me to board the trains, I bow and quickly fall into place. I never disrupt the flow of the moving mob. I accept that, in their eyes, I am a Jap girl. I notice that some of my prison friends at Tulare are not coming with us to the Gila River Camp. When I turn to Father Kawakita, he quickly looks down, and I know this is a signal to not ask aloud.

*   *   *

On August 27, 1942, we arrive at the Gila River Camp and are immediately assigned a sixteen-by-twenty-foot section in a barracks. Yes, 320 square feet for a family of three. We are issued three cots to sleep on, a few army-grade blankets, and a lightbulb. The outside temperature is in the triple digits, making the steamy heat inside our barracks unbearable.

The massive compound gives me pause. I am told there are over one thousand buildings on site. With a population of over thirteen thousand, the Gila River Camp is a large prison masquerading as a small city. I am surrounded by another fence (although there is no barbed wire) and one guard tower. But the four months in Tulare have prepared me for this experience.

While I am walking through the camp, my new best friend, Sachiko Miura, sees me and runs toward me so fast, I think she may not be able to stop in time.

"Mary," she says, "there is a rumor that the first lady, Eleanor Roosevelt, is coming to visit us. She was opposed to Executive Order 9066 and does not approve of these camps. Maybe after visiting us she can convince her husband to change everything back to the way it was."

When she stops to catch her breath, I say, "Sachiko, not likely."

Her excitement fading into a sad frown, she walks away, and I continue my walk. I am disgusted by what I see. Many others have described the Japanese internment war camps, and I concur that conditions are horrible.

Despite our grim surroundings, within the first three months there, I find my dignity, build strong personal bonds, and gain a better understanding of myself and how resilient I am. And, most importantly, I gain a much deeper appreciation for the freedom I have lost as an American citizen. This is my camp prison story.

From my memoirs (no date):
Boredom in camp is a plague. People must keep occupied and entertain themselves, so recreation programs are started: games, crafts, lessons, and talent shows.

Today, I am ironing in our small, partitioned room and singing my favorite songs. My neighbor, without my knowledge, asks the recreation head to listen. After hearing me, he pushes back the blanket that forms our imaginary wall and asks me to sing in a talent show. I am dumbfounded but agree to try. On a large stage built for the camp shows, I fearfully make my singing debut. I receive compliments and unexpected attention.

After this event, my life quickly changes.

From my memoirs (no date):
The quiet, gentle, nice boys are afraid to approach me. Instead, I meet the brash and bold ones. Among

them is a shy but loud young man, Setsuji Okumoto. He is unsure of himself, but determined to woo me. When he proposes marriage, I am taken aback by his boldness, but I like his courage and direct approach. Also, his friend

Set-chan in deep thought

Thomas is highly intelligent and humorous, a real gentleman—I have a lot of respect for Thomas, and his word that Setsuji is a good boy carries weight. I feel deep down there is a lonely and love-starved individual in Setsuji. He offers a special kinship. We both have gone through moments of terrible loneliness.

Set-chan (Setsuji is too formal; I now call him Set-chan as an endearment) was born in Loomis (near Sacramento), California, in 1914. His mother died four years later, during the 1918 Spanish Flu epidemic, and his father was unable to care for him and his sister. So, at the age of four, Set-chan and his sister were sent back to Hiroshima, Japan. There, his grandmother raised the two children. Like me, at an early age, he was given away. We share this common bond of abandonment and are building a trust between us that we hope will shelter our children from this ever happening to them.

When she grew up, Set-chan's sister came to America as a picture bride. During the early 1900s, Japanese women in Japan submitted pictures of themselves to Japanese suitors in America as possible marriage prospects. Once a woman was selected, she was married by proxy and then traveled to this country as a new Japanese bride. When Set-chan was nineteen years old, she sponsored him so he could come back to America.

Set-chan and I find each other in a time when the world is in chaos and our personal lives are in disarray. We rise above the noise of war and find a haven in the freezing temperatures of the Arizona desert. In November 1942, after a thirty-day whirlwind courtship, we promise that we will never leave each other.

> **From my memoirs (no date):**
> *The news of my engagement gets around and starts a chain reaction. My girlfriend who works in the mess hall (we call it our eating hall) tells me a fellow asked her if I am really getting married. When she said yes, he sat for a long time in a daze, and my friend felt extremely uncomfortable and sorry for him.*
>
> *Another talented and quite brainy young man once asked for my hand in marriage, but he is not my type and I refused him. Since then, I have avoided him at every turn. When he hears of my impending marriage, he begins to do strange things. He writes letters to the president of our country, saying that it is wrong to get into this war and many people will be harmed. How true that is—so many people's lives have been turned upside down. Unfortunately, he is eventually sent to an institution outside of camp.*

Leading up to our November 25 wedding, I capture this history:

> **From my bride's book (November 20–22, 1942):**
> *November 20, 1942—Set-chan put the engagement ring on my finger. I kiss the ring gently, thinking of the beloved one whose fingers have touched it.*

November 22, 1942—At the bridal shower. It is a surprise—I thought it was a gathering to arrange flowers for the mess hall. I am scared out of my wits when an alarm clock sitting among the gifts goes off.

About twenty-five friends, along with Mother and Father Kawakita, join Set-chan and me to witness our wedding vows on November 25, at 63 Buddhist Church in the Gila River Camp, with a reception afterward in Mess Hall 63. The first on the list is my close friend, Sachiko Miura.

The wedding gifts range from money (anywhere from $0.50 to $5.00) to articles of clothing and whatever else could be salvaged from the minimal belongings of our war camp–dwelling friends. The amounts we receive are ironic; we left behind many acres of valuable land, treasured possessions, and years of sweat and toil. (Ultimately, the government does pay internees about $38.5 million in reparations. Yet, per the Federal Reserve Bank of San Francisco, in 1942 the estimated value of our cumulative lost property is about $400 million. This excludes lost wages, interest, and appreciation on what is now some of the most valuable land on the West Coast. I can't imagine what that property is worth today—in today's dollars, possibly over $45 billion.)

Set-chan and Tome on their wedding day

More from my bride's book (November 25–
December 3, 1942):

*November 25, 1942—After the wedding and recep-
tion, we stay in the honeymoon cottage (Barrack
42-2-c). Very nicely furnished . . . really wish the
furniture belonged to us.*

*November 28, 1942—Move today into our long-term
cozy little home (Barrack 44-3-c). Home is really a
sweet place. Especially when it is shared with the
one you treasure in your heart.*

*December 3, 1942—Have our first guests. Must
start to expect guests often now.*

* * *

Then comes the loyalty oath in 1943.

I talk with several people about the loyalty oath questionnaire and discover they are being reclassified as disloyal
to the United States. They are being sent to the Tule Lake
Camp, a facility resembling a maximum-security prison.
This reclassification is born from answering "no" to two
questions, #27 and #28, on the loyalty questionnaire:

Question #27: Are you willing to serve in the armed
forces of the United States on combat duty, wherever
ordered?

Question #28: Will you swear unqualified allegiance
to the United States of America and faithfully defend
the United States from any and all attacks by foreign
or domestic forces, and forswear any form of allegiance to the Japanese Emperor or any other foreign
government, power, or organization?

Question #28 is especially troubling for Japanese migrants—United States law does not allow them to be naturalized citizens, but answering "yes" means they could lose their Japanese citizenship and become people without a country. Furthermore, the word *forswear* implies they had a previous allegiance to the Japanese emperor, and answering "yes" would make them enemies of the state.

This is a stupid, no-win situation. The "no-no boys"—the men who answer "no" to both questions—refuse to fight for a country that denies them the very rights they are fighting for. Some say *Shikata ga nai* ("Things can't be helped" or "Let it go"). By standing up for themselves, they are rewarded with felony jail time in state penitentiaries. We have lost our freedom and been oppressed and denied our rights as American citizens. Now, we are prosecuted.

To put this in perspective, of the approximately 110,000 Japanese Americans who have been incarcerated without due process of law, about 70,000 are American citizens like Set-chan and me. Our only crime is our Japanese ancestry and physical appearance; we are disdained as visual immigrants. (Ironically, no Japanese American or Japanese national is ever found guilty of sabotage or espionage.)

Adding more insult to this travesty, in 1944 the military draft is reinstated, and Japanese American boys and men are drafted into the United States military. Those who avoid or disregard their draft notices are jailed. Imagine leaving your parents incarcerated while you fight a war for the people who imprisoned you and your relatives.

Many young Japanese American men do volunteer. They do this to prove their loyalty to their new home, America. These are the great men of the 442nd Regimental Combat

Team and the 100th Infantry Battalion. Like them, I am determined to come out of this as a stronger American. What I don't understand, if the disloyal Japanese Americans are now identified and have been sent to a high-security prison, why am I and other identified loyal Americans still imprisoned? This is so frustrating.

*   *   *

On February 2, 1944, my world changes. I become a mother.

> **From my memoirs (no date):**
> *After my marriage I do not sing in public anymore. Our first child is born in camp. There aren't many babies, so she is the center of attention among our friends and neighbors.*

From 1944 through 1945, while I am busy caring for a newborn, I don't walk the camp as much as before, but Sachiko keeps me informed.

One afternoon she stops by. "Mary, I was told there is a monument on the top of the hill just past our row of barracks. Let's go see it."

"Really? Let me grab my daughter and let's take the hike."

At the top of the hill is a monument that lists the names of Japanese American soldiers who have lost their lives in battle. I find the names of several of my high school friends. After that initial visit, I periodically come back to check the list. Every time, the list grows longer. I become more aware of the emotional agony and personal losses suffered by my camp friends, communicated in blood-soaked, tear-stained letters from sons and brothers fighting in Europe.

In July 1945, I am eight months pregnant with my second daughter. On August 6, 1945, the first atomic bomb is dropped on Japan. The second atomic bomb is dropped three days later. These two bombs instantly kill more people than everyone who is incarcerated in the Japanese war camps in America. Unfortunately, many more will die after the bombing due to radiation exposure. Six days after these bombings, the Empire of Japan officially surrenders to the Allied Forces. One week and one day later, my second daughter's cries echo through a partially vacant war camp.

Late one afternoon I see Set-chan standing in the corner of the infirmary, weeping. His body is limp and bent over, as if he is carrying a heavy load. But when he looks up and sees me lying with our new daughter, he smiles peacefully.

Standing by my bedside is a nurse with a letter from Father Kawakita. I point out Set-chan to her, and she whispers, "Tome, Setsuji is in mourning. The first atomic bomb was dropped on Hiroshima, where Setsuji grew up. His school friends, his grandmother who raised him, and his relatives were maimed or killed. All the places he remembers from his youth have been destroyed."

I look beyond the nurse and at Set-chan. While drowning in the sorrow of his personal loss, he still manages to summon a smile, projecting his hope for us. At this moment I understand his strength.

I open the letter. Father Kawakita's short note reads, "Take care of Setsuji, Tome. You are his family now. He and all of your current and future children are your duty, your *ikigai*."

On September 2, 1945, representatives of the Japanese government sign a surrender document aboard the battleship USS *Missouri*—Japan is officially defeated. A month later we are packed and prepared to leave camp. Mother and Father Kawakita have already driven back to Southern California. Set-chan and I have plans for our new life elsewhere.

As I stand at the camp's entry gates, the fall winds toss my hair across my face. I see myself as a stranger in this land. I came here as a young and naïve Jap girl. I am no longer ashamed of being that person, no longer bear the false guilt of having done something wrong. I understand the courage I have gained during the time I was incarcerated, and I am leaving now, three and a half years later, as a wife, a mother, and an American. These gifts reflect how breakage in my life created golden lines of beauty, my family.

I hold the hand of my older daughter while cradling my newborn, keeping them close so they can hear my promise to them: "As your mother, I promise to protect you from becoming prisoners in your own country again." I hold my head high and promise myself I will never again be a victim. Looking down at the fine-grained dirt that invaded every part of my life, I take my first step once again as a free person.

8

Freedom, Samurai, and American Heroes

We receive twenty-five dollars each and a train ticket home. Only, there is no home to go to. Set-chan and I discuss where we might live, and all options rely on his relatives. We choose his cousin, Big George. He has a produce farm on the outskirts of Salt Lake City, Utah, where we are more likely to find work. So, with our small family we trek to Salt Lake City in the frosty autumn of 1945 to find home.

When we arrive at Big George's home, his welcoming family greets us with open hearts, a warm fire, and a meal of rice and fish. The aroma of Japanese food cooking settles my nerves and relaxes my body tension built up from our long journey. We spend our first night sharing camp stories, then sleeping on the living room floor. Tomorrow we will move into the empty chicken coop behind the house.

Early the next morning, Big George and Set-chan move our belongings into the chicken coop. After everything is moved, I start nesting, making the coop our new home.

———

"I found an old crib and placed it in the center of the coop, close to the stove," Big George says. "You'll find firewood around back. We gathered surplus army blankets and placed them next to the crib inside. I know it's not much, but we'll find more to help you settle in."

I bow to Big George. "Thank you. Thank you so much for having us. Set-chan and I are deeply grateful for you taking us in."

Big George smiles, grabs Set-chan, and leads him to the truck. They drive off to find work, and I see that relatives are watching over the girls in the main house. I take advantage of this free time to enter the coop. After scanning every corner, I quickly realize the most important thing I must do is address the chill. The girls need a much warmer environment. When I exhale, white vapors circle my face.

In the center of the coop is a wood-burning potbellied stove. It reminds me of the one we had on the chicken farm. I step outside, walk around to the back of the coop, and find a neatly stacked cord of very dry wood. I pick up three pieces and cradle them in my arms so I can carry them to the coop. As I place them into the potbellied stove, I picture a blazing fire. I ignite the kindling, which crackles, creating an initial warmth. I work the air damper to properly size the fire for warmth and longer burn duration.

Mesmerized by the sight of our first three logs burning in the stove, I reflect upon my days on the chicken farm and Mother telling me, "Never let the fire go out. There is an art to keeping the fire lit all day or all night." She explained why certain hard woods should be used for the stove, how the air damper works, and the importance of ash and kindling. I look up and thank Mother for teaching me about wood-burning stoves.

I busily pile blankets and our extra clothing on top of the cots to keep us warm during the night. I stuff the wooden crib with old coats and jackets, neatly folding them so they are safely positioned for our newborn.

The fading sunlight of my first full day is accompanied by the sound of Big George's truck rolling into the yard. Stepping outside, I see Big George and Set-chan laughing. Their smiles bring me such joy.

Set-chan comes up to me, beaming with happiness. "I got a job at night washing dishes in the Hotel Utah, and Big George says he will pay me to drive his produce-hauling truck to make deliveries during the day."

I bow to Big George and say, "Thank you." He blushes and invites us to dinner in the big house tonight. A sense of belonging and family brings a calm into my heart. Again, I bow and thank Big George.

During dinner, Big George and Set-chan chatter about the beauty and luxury of the Hotel Utah. I want to see it. Having grown up in Southern California farm country, I have not seen anything as magnificent as their description of the Hotel Utah.

The next afternoon, after driving the produce truck all day, Set-chan runs to the bus stop to catch a ride to work in the hotel. When early evening arrives, I tell Big George I need to take dinner to Set-chan at the hotel, as it is his first night working there. He smiles, knowing I am curious. After he explains the bus transfers to get to the Hotel Utah, I scurry off and quickly pack a dinner for Set-chan. Bundling into several layers of clothes, I look up, imagining my first adventure as a newlywed.

After arriving at the hotel, I find the back entrance and drop off Set-chan's food. Then I leave the kitchen area and wander through a maze of hallways. A large double door opens to a restaurant, and I cautiously make my way to another wide hallway, trying not to be noticed. Facing me is a large archway; I walk through it and find myself standing in a magnificent lobby. I overhear a distinguished-looking couple describing the architectural firm, based in both Salt Lake City and Los Angeles, that designed the hotel. I am proud to hear that a firm from my hometown produced such a masterpiece. A sudden "humph" erupts from a gentleman in a black suit standing in front of me.

"I am so sorry, I lost my way. Which way is it to the lobby?"

"Young lady, you are in the lobby. Please exit down that hall. That will take you to the service entrance. You may leave through that door."

"Thank you."

I slowly walk down the hall in that direction, but when I peek over my shoulder the gentleman is gone. I quickly turn around and head back toward the lobby. Before leaving, I want to catch a glimpse of the grand lobby with its rich, dark flooring, and maybe even walk through it. I hope one day I might book a stay. Of course, I know this is just a fantasy— nonwhites are not allowed to stay at the hotel.

Someday one of my girls will have the honor and the good fortune to stay as guests at the Hotel Utah. I can live my fantasy through their experience. I traverse the lobby unnoticed, exit through the front doors, and turn to face the ten-story hotel. It is a warm haven compared to the frosty night outside. But no matter the cold, I look up, mesmerized by the large white dome that graces the top of this magnificent structure. Standing next to this masterpiece on the corner of Main and South Temple, I feel like royalty. I hate to leave, but I need to get home to the girls and put them to bed.

I hurry to the bus stop, the bitter cold stripping away any warmth I had garnered inside. A hiss of smoke and steam announces my bus rolling up and reminds me of my place in life. As the bus doors open, I step aboard and fumble in my coat pocket, looking for the correct change.

The next day, through recommendations from Set-chan's relatives, I find work cleaning homes and weeding in a farmer's spinach field across the street. Fortunately, Set-chan's relatives also volunteer to take turns caring for the girls. With both of us working, life is very good. My only regret is that we live in a converted chicken coop, facing direct exposure to the harsh elements of winter. I am always cold. We must fully dress the girls before they can go to bed. And every night after his shift at the Hotel Utah, Set-chan shivers for hours. We need a change. All winter we discuss where we can go to find better weather.

On the first sunny day in the spring of 1946, Set-chan and I prepare for our long drive to a new home in a warmer climate. Set-chan's sister moved to Pasadena, in Southern California, after the war. My foster parents are also renting an apartment in Southern California. Having relatives there makes the decision easy.

This morning Big George waits for us by our new used car. "Setsuji and Tome, we will miss you and the girls. Please write us and keep in touch."

He bows, and we respond with deeper bows.

"Thank you for taking us in and helping us find work. We will never forget you," Set-chan says softly in Japanese.

Big George then turns to me and extends both hands. "Tome, please accept this folding map of Southern California. It is a bit weathered, but it will help guide you to your parents' home."

I gently grasp the crumpled, water-stained map and bow to Big George. "Thank you for this map and your generosity. We will never forget you. You helped us find our freedom again, and now we must find our home."

In unison, we tread lightly to our car. Set-chan opens the driver's side door and sits down on the bench seat. Our eldest daughter sits between Set-chan and me, and I cradle my baby girl, keeping her head safe from any sharp movements. Set-chan turns the key in the ignition, and the engine immediately rumbles, acknowledging its readiness to take us to our new life. Another fresh start. My heart misses the safety of our chicken coop, but my dreams wish for much more in Southern California. Still, en route, fear of the unknown pulses through my body, causing me to shiver.

The return address on Mother and Father Kawakita's letters directs us to an apartment in Los Angeles County. Studying the map with its multiple folds, I chart our course. Before the war, the Los Angeles neighborhood of San Pedro was home to a mammoth fishing industry. It makes sense that my parents have resettled there—Father Kawakita can find work in the fishing industry.

When we arrive at the small apartment complex, I shudder. Their apartment is embedded inside a run-down, rat-infested building that reeks of rotting food, or much worse. We exit our car and the girls yawn and tug at me, wanting to go to the bathroom. Set-chan and I scour the complex, looking for my parents' apartment number. We find it and cautiously walk up to the door. The stench is so strong that I cover my mouth and nose. The girls continue to fidget, signaling they need to relieve themselves.

Upon reaching the apartment door, I knock with force. I hear someone inside shuffling toward us. Then the door opens abruptly and Mother leaps at me and hugs me. She mumbles something while crying on my shoulder. I see how harsh the war has been to her, robbing her of life itself. She no longer projects the image of a disciplinarian, and although I feel her warmth when I hold her, the stern rigidity is gone. Standing in front of me is a shadow of a beaten soul.

Mother invites us in and immediately bursts out in her accented English, "I am so happy to see you and Setsuji. I have been living alone for months, starving and afraid. Father got a job working as a cook on a commercial fishing boat. At fifty-nine, he is doing anything he can to survive."

"Momma, I need to go to the bathroom." A big scream from a little girl. Set-chan asks where it is and then carries our eldest in that direction.

My joy at finding Mother is marred by her stories of post-camp life. No longer living in fresh air and sunshine, no longer working honestly on open acres of land, my foster parents are subsisting in the squalor of the indigent and forgotten.

"Father is a proud and humble man," Mother repeats, "who no longer casts his noble shadow. With the war behind us, he has lost his coat of armor and cannot protect me from the outside world." Then, suddenly, as if the girls have been invisible until now, she says, "Tome and Setsuji, my grandkids are so beautiful. Please get your things from the car."

We carry our meager belongings from our car into the apartment. Scanning the living room, I realize there is very little furniture. Such a contrast to our home in Gardena before the war. Set-chan, the girls, and I sleep on the floor for the first few weeks.

Although our temporary home is cramped, I love the warm weather and sharing life with Mother. In the early mornings I walk outside to look beyond our small street and see distant mountains. I lift my head and breathe in the air of freedom, living without barbed wire or the shadows of military sentries controlling the physical borders of our lives.

The end of summer comes quickly. Set-chan and I agree it is time we find a house and move everyone out of the apartment. But in the wake of the war, we cannot escape being disdained as visual immigrants, and many people refuse to rent to us, citing their "rule" of not renting to families with young children. Set-chan and I bow and graciously accept the excuses as we watch white families take our spot, kids

Tome at 60 Yale Street

and all. I am again reminded: Because I look different, I am not accepted as an American.

Our next option is to buy a small house. On a sweltering Indian summer day, we visit Set-chan's relatives, the Shimodas, in Pasadena. As we are leaving, Set-chan says, "We love your home. We are looking for a small house, but no one will rent to us or sell us one. A realtor I know let it slip that we are 'redlined' out of many areas, especially the nice areas that are white-only."

"Setsuji, our neighbor is selling their home," Set-chan's cousin says. "They are a kindly German couple who will empathize with your dilemma. I know they will agree to sell you their house."

Without hesitation we walk to the house, knock on the front door, and are greeted by an older couple. They remind me of the Weises, our neighbors in Gardena before the war. After a whirlwind of several days, we step into our first house at 60 Yale Street assisted by sympathetic seller financing. It is a small, two-bedroom home with one bathroom. I love it.

* * *

While unpacking boxes at our new home, Mother finds unopened letters from Japan. Paralyzed, she holds them, then stares at me.

"Mother, why haven't you opened these letters?" I ask.

After a long pause, she says, "Tome, they are from Father's parents. I cannot bear to open them. I know they hate me. I know they feel I stole their son. I know they view me as a commoner and not worthy of their son. I know they consider me just a poor farmer and below their noble class."

"Please read them. I want to know about Japan and what's happening there."

Looking tortured, Mother acquiesces, opens a letter, and reads aloud in Japanese, "Fude"—Mother's first name—"I want my son to know that we are alive. We are starving and our beautiful home near Kumamoto Castle has been ravaged and lies barren. Our lives are bleak and depressing. Constant reminders of August 9, 1945, ring in my ears, from air raid sirens to the explosion of the atomic bomb in the neighboring prefecture of Nagasaki. Our son, Yoshitsugu"—Father Kawakita's first name—"must come home to Japan and help us. We are battling famine and endless fatigue. He must honor us. We demand his loyalty. He must do what prior Kawakita generations have always done and accept the family katana." Mother stops, reads no more, and walks away.

A chill runs down my spine. It is clear that people living in Japan during the occupation have it much worse than us.

Without telling anyone, Mother begins sending dried foods and money to Father Kawakita's parents in Japan. One sunset, Mother receives a letter from them. It is their last correspondence. Mother never shares these letters with Father Kawakita. I am not sure why.

*   *   *

In the spring of 1947, a few months after we move into the Yale Street house, our neighborhood breaks into celebration. A young baseball player who grew up a few blocks from our new house, Jackie Robinson, has become the first Black American player in Major League Baseball. When they describe Robinson's childhood neighborhood as impoverished, I say to myself, *So this is what poverty looks like.* Before the war and during the Great Depression, we were spared economic chaos thanks to our chickens and eggs.

Now, I tell Set-chan, "We only have ourselves to barter...a reminder that life can change without notice."

Set-chan, looking amused, says, "A *nisei*—a firstborn Japanese American child and a United States citizen, like us—bartered his life in the Hotel Utah this year. I received a letter from Big George telling me that a local Japanese American basketball player, Wat Misaka, signed his professional basketball contract with the New York Knicks at the Hotel Utah. He's the first nonwhite professional basketball player in the Basketball Association of America." Stunned, I shake my head. Set-chan is making up another story. A Japanese American professional basketball player? No way. Set-chan walks away, laughing, knowing he is telling the truth.

Shortly after these 1947 celebrations we receive the gift of our first son. Set-chan and I are incredibly happy that the Okumoto name will live on through him. The addition of a new child, combined with my foster parents moving in with us, initiates the idea that we need a bigger house. Working as a family, we begin saving money for a down payment. Collectively, we save enough for a larger home around the corner. There, our fourth child is born. We name him Richard. Set-chan and I feel richer—now we have two sons to carry on our family name.

Not long after Richard is born, I find and connect with my younger sisters, June and Kiku. June is married to a Hawaiian boy from Hilo, and Kiku is still single. Having more family around erases the many years of loneliness I felt as an only child.

June is well suited to her role as auntie to my four kids. She loves impromptu visits, and today, a mild day in the late summer of 1952, is no exception. A knock sounds at the back door and June enters the house, bent over and out of breath, and immediately sits down at the kitchen table. Perspiration covers her face, and she is barely able to speak. As she tries to take in a deep breath, I stop cooking and gaze at her.

"Mary, the government just passed a law," she says, her eyes opening wide, "that will allow our parents to become naturalized US citizens."

I am surprised and relieved by her news.

"It's called the McCarran–Walter Act," June continues, her breathing now back to normal. "It expands the first Naturalization Act passed by Congress in 1790. The 1790 act set the rules for naturalization—only 'free, White persons' of 'good character' who had been residents for two years or more were eligible. It effectively excluded Native Americans, indentured servants, enslaved persons, free Blacks, and Orientals."

Until now, ten years after they were incarcerated in the war camps, my foster parents could not become naturalized American citizens. Of course, even if they had been citizens when the war broke out, it would not have mattered. I was a US citizen, and I was incarcerated. What amazes me is that Native Americans could not become US citizens until 1924, fifty-six years after African Americans were granted US citizenship with the ratification of the Fourteenth Amendment.

Finally, there are political changes that improve our family's life. We are benefiting from the 1950s Golden Era: excellent economic conditions, the eradication of such diseases as polio, and more progressive attitudes toward Orientals. I feel blessed for the positive direction.

June smiles and prepares to leave. "I've got to go and see some friends to tell them the good news." I hear her talking to herself as she dashes out the back door and almost trips down our porch steps.

I take a deep breath and say aloud, "Life is good."

Shortly thereafter, Set-chan enters the kitchen, surprising me.

"What are you doing home so early?"

He grins deeply, unable to contain his excitement, and says, "I found the perfect corner lot on which we can build our new house. I shook hands with the seller and his agent. It is in a decent neighborhood that we have been redlined out of . . . and it can be ours."

How did Set-chan bypass the redlining?

"Tome, when I first saw this corner lot, I knew the owners would not sell it to me if they thought I was going to build our home on it. When they asked what I did for work, I mentioned I own a nursery and do gardening. The agent said the lot was zoned for both residential and commercial. I immediately told them I am looking to expand my nursery, and this would be a great step up. The corner lot is over a quarter acre and would be perfect for expanding my business."

He stands in front of me, waiting for my response. I am in shock.

Set-chan continues, "We have the lot to build our new home."

So, in 1955, we purchase the ideal corner lot. With help from our relatives, we build our new home. Once it is completed, Set-chan focuses fiercely on paying off the mortgage in seven years. He does not want to be in a situation where the government can seize it. Fear of what happened before the war lingers, and his constant distrust of unknown government powers keeps him fixed on our finances.

* * *

As world events continue improving our lives, Obaachan (what we now call Mother, as it means "grandmother" in Japanese) becomes gravely ill. During the next few weeks, I spend many hours sitting by her bedside, learning about her life. I finally garner enough courage to ask about my real mom. Obaachan becomes visibly uncomfortable.

Uncharacteristically softly, she says in her accented English, "Tome, my time is short. I always wanted to tell you about your mother, but I did not find the right time. I guess it is now." Obaachan takes an unsteady breath. "I don't know your real mother, Mina, very well. Unlike me, a picture bride, she was betrothed to my older brother, Tekeichi, when they were living in Saga Prefecture. Like the picture brides, they were married by proxy in Japan, which enabled her to enter America.

"Your mother trained to be a midwife and hoped to practice in this country. But my brother is fifteen years older than Mina and wanted children immediately. Saddled with raising their nine kids, less you, and working nine hours a day on the farm left her no time to be a midwife. Her life as a farmer's wife was bleak and quickly aged her. She is now tortured by her arthritic hands and back, and walks hunched over."

From my memoirs (no date):

After many bedside conversations, I observe Obaachan's gradual decline and loss of her tough, direct demeanor. On her last night, I admit that I love her. I bend over her and tell her, "You are and will always be my mom." After I deliver these words, she closes her eyes and displays a seldom-seen smile. Over her lifetime, I now realize, she gave me her love and shared her dreams with me and for me. The next morning, July 18, 1958, at 8 a.m., Obaachan departs, leaving a big hole in my life. She is only sixty-four years old (she was born on March 25, 1894) when she passes away.

Before and after Obaachan's funeral, cards and letters of condolence flood our mailbox. Her passing brings together relatives and camp friends from all over the world. It is amazing how a tight-knit community grew out of our degrading experience in the United States Japanese war camps. I feel so lost without her—she was my rock.

One month after Obaachan's passing, I notice Ojiichan (what we now call Father Kawakita, as it means "grandfather" in Japanese) sitting by our pond, looking up at the sky. His stoic face has lost its familiarity, and I realize I know very little about him. What I do know about Ojiichan's life before he came to America is that he lived the way of the samurai, Bushido. I want to learn more about his life, having missed so much of Obaachan's.

At our next breakfast, when Ojiichan and I are sitting alone at the kitchen table, I say, "Ojiichan, you are my family.

I missed so much of Obaachan's life. Please consider sharing your life story with me."

Ojiichan's baldness accentuates his impassive face and eyes. He offers a small smile and speaks comfortingly. "Tome, we will talk each morning before you go to work." With a sheepish grin, he adds, "You remind me of a great woman samurai named Tomoe Gozen. Yes, there were women samurai, and many were fierce warriors. I am not sure if she was real, but her legend reminds me of you."

When asked, he opens a door into his heart. Why had I not asked either Obaachan or Ojiichan before?

"I know I do not have many years ahead of me," he continues. "I want to share with you our lost legacy.... Let us start with my full name, Yoshitsugu Kawakita. I was born on July 2, 1887."

I quiver as I watch him and hear his story unfold.

* * *

Each morning before going to work, I sit with Ojiichan and listen to his stories of growing up in a military family in Japan. The discipline, the rigor of his mental and physical training, which was both grueling and cleansing. He always adopts a gentle tone, offsetting the strictness of his childhood.

He starts by telling me about the foundational principles of Bushido, and the last samurai. "Ten years before I was born, the battle of the last samurai took place. Saigo Takamori was the last samurai. The samurai rebellions occurred between 1874 and 1877, after the actual samurai class was dissolved in 1868. This coincides with the end of the Edo period in Japan. The samurai were reduced to *shizoku,* with no special class privileges. Yet we, the *shizoku* military class, still embraced Bushido—the foundation of honor, courage, compassion, respect, integrity, loyalty, self-control, and strict discipline."

Every day thereafter, we chat before I leave for work. Certain discussions stand out more than others, such as this one:

"Tome, through our years together you have been exposed to the way of the warrior—Bushido. The world has changed since those earlier times, maybe for the better. Bushido is no longer the way of the warrior, but has become the way of the people, *Mindo*. Before coming to America, I studied a book published in 1908 called *Bushido: The Soul of Japan*, written in Japanese by Dr. Nitobe. I agree with his stance on this matter."

His stories eventually stray away from the broad strokes of his upbringing and philosophy and lead to more personal details. Finally, one morning, Ojiichan opens his heart, sharing private moments that lie deep in his memories of home.

"Tome, today I will talk about my life in Kumamoto. My life was centered around Kumamoto Castle, where samurai were a prominent part of our ancestry and history. One samurai, Musashi Miyamoto—a great samurai, maybe the greatest samurai—spent his final years living close to my home in Kumamoto. A giant of a samurai at nearly six feet tall, he towered over other samurais, some of whom were barely taller than five feet.

He was a skilled swordsman and never lost a fight. Living among nature and close to his good friend Hosokawa, another samurai, this great samurai crafted notes about applying Bushido to other contexts, adding to his legacy. As a student, I learned of his work through elders in the prefecture, and his life inspired me to become more than who I was. He died on June 13, and that day is marked with sadness and remembrance of a great soul."

Ojiichan continues his stories about this great samurai and interjects his conflicted emotions over never returning to Kumamoto, thus abandoning his heritage. As he describes Kumamoto Castle, he begins to tear up and abruptly stops and walks away.

As the years pass, I notice subtle changes in Ojiichan. We talk less and he retreats into a quiet place. What doesn't change is his love for the Japanese game of Go. It is the rawest form of battle: black versus white player pieces, good versus evil, right versus wrong. It is this clarity and simplicity that makes the game powerful and complex.

One day, in 1960, Ojiichan receives a letter from relatives in Kumamoto. It states that more than ten years ago, in 1947, the Japanese civil code eliminated the *shizoku* class, formerly the samurai class, officially erasing the samurai class in Japan. This letter suggests that Ojiichan has nothing left at home in Japan, no legacy. Proud and broken, he descends into a valley of sadness. What else will be taken from him?

He walks outside and sits at a small card table on the concrete patio that stretches between the kitchen and one bedroom. Then, in a rare emotional moment, he screams at the world he reentered beyond the barbed-wire fences and sweeps the black-and-white pieces off the solid-wood Go board. As they scatter throughout the backyard and into the nearby pond, Ojiichan cries aloud. He rubs his eyes, and his hands become moist from his tears.

The simple truth of his current situation is painfully self-evident. In a country that is foreign to him, he is alone, save for his adopted family. I constantly remind him that he is my family. He raised me, we survived a world war, and we will survive future challenges together. Ojiichan reminds me of the Japanese American warriors of World War II, the soldiers of the 442nd and the 100th Battalions.

My younger sister June's husband was a member of the 100th Battalion, made up of Hawaiian-born Japanese American men. In August 1944, the 100th joined together with the stateside Japanese American men and boys who made up the 442nd Regimental Combat Team. The 442nd and the 100th were legendary World War II fighters who collectively displayed exemplary loyalty to America. This group of Japanese American men was the most decorated unit in history for its size and length of service. Their famous battle cry, "Go for broke," lives to this day.

In 1961, at a fourth-grade Washington Elementary School PTA (parent-teacher association) meeting, I see a good friend, Mrs. Ichino, standing in a corner alone and walk up to her. She smiles, recognizing a friendly face. We talk about our sons, Richard and Ted, who are in the same class and love hearing stories about the war. She mentions that her husband, Frank, was a sergeant in the Army and a member of the 442nd.

"During one of Frank's many angry moods," Mrs. Ichino says, "he muttered something about an October 1944 battle in France, during which two regiments had failed to extricate Texas soldiers who were pinned down and surrounded by German soldiers. Frank said a bunch of Texans thought they could single-handedly take on the entire German army, and now they were cut off. Then this general [Dahlquist] looks around and says, 'Hell, we've got these traitorous Japs sitting around; let's throw them at the Germans and make it look like we tried to get them out.'"

I shudder and remind myself this is 1961 and not 1944. My mind drifts and I wonder, *Are times different now? Maybe not.*

Mrs. Ichino continues Frank's story. "They were strung out so thin that they couldn't see the guy in front of or behind them. They'd been getting chopped up by a German machine gun. Suddenly these two Germans came running out of the brush carrying replacement belts for the machine gun. Frank shot one in the head and scattered fire into some bushes that the other guy dove into."

"Was Frank sorry about killing those soldiers?" I ask.

Mrs. Ichino lowers her voice and tells me what Frank told her. "He said, 'It was him or me. It was something that had to be done—I'm not proud of it, but I'm not ashamed of it either. You know, most of the soldiers in World War II—on both sides—grew up on farms. Once you've butchered a hog as a teenager, you can do things that would give a city boy nightmares.'"

After the honesty of that moment, Mrs. Ichino looks down, attempting to escape the memories of that day. "Frank said they [442nd L Company] went up the mountain at combat strength. Only seven of them walked off it; four went to the infirmary. Over a hundred men started out, and he was one of the three left standing."

For a few moments, we stare at each other in silence. Instinctively, I step forward and give her a hug. "Please tell Frank I appreciate his bravery and the honor he brought to all of us."

What I discover, after talking to camp friends, is that the Japanese American soldiers of the 442nd broke through German lines and saved the Texas Lost Battalion. Various accounts of that battle include such statistics as hundreds of Japanese American soldiers losing their lives to save the two hundred Texans. The accuracy of these accounts is open for discussion.

What *is* true is that five Medals of Honor were awarded to the Japanese American soldiers of the 442nd for their bravery during the battle for the Lost Battalion. What *is* true is that in 1962, Texas Governor John Connally made the veterans of the 442nd honorary Texans.

Like so many of those brave, young Japanese American soldiers who died and left behind family, Ojiichan leaves me orphaned on May 3, 1962.

That morning, at 8:30 a.m., a loud *thud* from the back porch alerts me to come running from my bedroom to see what has happened. I find Ojiichan lying listlessly on the linoleum floor. His stoic expression has been replaced by a peaceful smile.

He whispers, "Tome, thank you for being my daughter. Thank you for being my legacy. I raised you the only way I knew how, living Bushido. I hope you will hold on to your life lessons. When I adopted you, when I gave you my name, Kawakita, you became my family...."

I cradle his head as he gasps, "Tome ... *kokoro*." Then he takes his final breath.

There, on that cold floor, I am crushed by my personal loss. I break the promise I made to myself as a six-year-old Jap girl—his passing shatters my heart.

His departure is followed in the fall of that year by Set-chan's screams of pain. In 1962, after twenty years of marriage, I face the challenge of poverty alone. What will I do? I am not prepared.

9

The Other America

My journey through the cultural revolution of the 1960s, which moves at dizzying speeds, is a challenging one. It starts in mid-1962, when I lose Ojiichan to a heart attack. Set-chan, the kids, and I sit in the front row of the Higashi Honganji Buddhist Temple in downtown Los Angeles, where we honor his life. I did not know then that my position in our family would shortly change.

Stories of his family military lineage call up visions of Ojiichan as a lost samurai: a *ronin* who has lost his master, or *daimyo*. How long did he wander, lost, before finding Mother? Can he now return to his forbidden place? Can he return home to Kumamoto, Japan? I pray that he can. I pray that he can now return home.

<blockquote>

From my memoirs (no date):

I recall the stories of Ojiichan's life with sadness. His parents had high hopes for him—their ancestors had been warriors of notable worth, and they expected him to become a great soldier or navy man. Because

</blockquote>

he had gotten poor grades in English, his father sent him to America to learn the language, securing him a position as an officers' cook on United States Coast and Geodetic Survey vessels. He served on the Explorer, the Gedney, and the Taku. Ojiichan loved the freedom of being on the ocean.

His father certainly did not expect him to live the rest of his life in America, for his destiny was to continue the Kawakita family tradition and name. Yet, having tasted freedom from uncomfortable traditions and obligations, Ojiichan was determined to never return to such a restricted life.

The Buddhist priest's chanting subsides to a low "*umm.*" The clicking sounds of the Buddhist prayer beads, *nenju*, maintain a steady beat as my heart pounds. It was only four years ago that I performed this same ritual at Obaachan's funeral.

I stand up and slowly walk toward the front of the temple. I clasp my hands together, bow, and reach into a dark urn filled with powdered incense. I pinch some between my fingers and, with a nervous and jerky motion of my right hand, flick it into a black cast-iron kettle that sits directly in front of Ojiichan's open casket. The incense fuels the smoldering flame within the kettle, producing a circular cloud in front of me.

I cough, the pungent aroma of burning incense trapped in my nostrils. The smell turns my stomach. Forever after that day, the scent of burning incense means to me that death is in the air. Ojiichan once said, "Tome, before battle, a samurai will place incense in their helmet, preparing for death."

We return home late in the afternoon. The kids scatter and Set-chan goes off to the Bellefontaine Nursery to see Frank about fixing his lawn mower—I think he is going to have a beer with Frank and the boys at the lawn mower shop. Alone, I open a dusty box filled with Ojjichan's prized possessions: an old ikebana *kenzan,* a teapot, a wooden ladle, a wooden whisk, a wooden spoon, and a packet filled with green powder. The word MATCHA is scribbled on it with an old felt pen. I haven't seen these items since we lived in Gardena before the war. Instantly, I know what to do.

Donning an old kimono, I carefully lay out the wooden tools, the teapot, and the green packet. My mind and body perform precise movements that result in hot tea whisked into a bright green foam in my tea bowl. I turn the bowl around and slowly sip the bitter tea, remembering that I should have prepared my mouth with something sweet to offset the harsh taste.

Like the samurai, who practiced Japanese tea ceremony to find calm in their lives, today I practice Japanese tea ceremony to find harmony and life balance. Preparing and consuming the tea quiets my mind while focusing my thoughts. With Ojiichan's passing, I break free of the shackles that have restricted my identity to that of just a daughter and wife. I have lost so much of myself over these past years—I need to find myself.

From my memoirs (no date):
I now understand, it is when you lose both parents that you finally become an adult. Shortly after Ojiichan's funeral I decide to find a job more suitable for me, one that has medical benefits. I apply

for a counselor position at an Oriental employment agency, Yamato. To my surprise, I am hired. After a few months of training, I settle into my job and into my own office.

Working at the Yamato Employment Agency gives me a renewed sense of pride, which I had lost during and after the war. I love helping others, and working in an office environment is invigorating.

*   *   *

Yamato is in downtown Los Angeles, and I have been commuting by bus. On a cool autumn evening in 1962, my son Richard is waiting for me at the bus stop on Fair Oaks Avenue. He has been running and is gasping for air, but manages to get out, "Mom . . . Mom, the Huntington Hospital has been calling and asking for you. It's about Dad."

I grab Richard's hand and walk briskly up to the house, muttering, "What else did they say?"

Richard shrugs. "Nothing else."

A hurricane has been unleashed. I am now running in knee-deep water, with gale-force winds pounding me from all sides.

From my memoirs (no date):
Just as things are going well, my world comes tumbling down. Set-chan and a friend are standing between two parked cars when an elderly woman loses control of her car and rams into the parked cars, trapping both men. They suffer leg injuries and are taken by ambulance to the hospital emergency room.

Set-chan has a double compound fracture of his right leg, and it is touch and go as to whether that leg will need to be amputated. He is in terror of losing it. The doctors try desperately to save it. I am grateful my parents are gone and do not witness these dark days.

In the wake of the accident, my husband enters a mental, physical, and emotional void. We are confronted with a bitter, frustrated, unreasonable, and deeply depressed patient. After the many operations to save his right leg, he is in great pain, and the continuous stream of painkillers drives Set-chan out of his mind.

His moods are unpredictable. His terrible fits of anger, then depression, turn him violent. He rants and raves and throws ashtrays or dishes at the boys and me. I tell the boys, "One should not judge a person when he is in great pain, for he doesn't know what he is doing." The boys are being so good, but I know it is leaving huge emotional scars.

Working at Yamato has been my dream job—I have been learning and growing there. But after the accident, I need to be physically closer to home. I must return to cleaning homes. My loyalty to Set-chan and my children outweighs my personal desires. My *ikigai* comes first.

*   *   *

In early 1963, one worklady—my respectful term for the women who hire me to clean their homes—suggests I read Michael Harrington's book *The Other America*. I visit

Vroman's Bookstore on Colorado Boulevard in Pasadena to find the book. Its dark cover with the author's name in red letters stands out on the bookstore shelves. But it is outside my budget and I cannot justify buying it.

This worklady, Mrs. Thompson, is the wife of a naval officer. She lives alone most of the time, and I sense her loneliness. So, after I clean her home, I often stay and chat. Every week Mrs. Thompson asks if I have read Harrington's book.

Not wanting to appear rude, I nod and say, "Yes, I will look into it."

One day, Mrs. Thompson asks, "Mary, why are you cleaning homes? You are too smart and inquisitive to be a domestic cleaning my house."

"Mrs. Thompson," I say, "my husband was in a terrible auto accident that crushed his right leg. I need to be physically close to home if an emergency arises."

At our next chat, after weeks of my vague answers about buying Harrington's book, it mysteriously appears next to my paycheck for cleaning the house.

I turn to her and say, "Mrs. Thompson, thank you."
She winks.

After I finish reading Harrington's book, Mrs. Thompson and I have several frank conversations about it.

"I now have a better understanding of poverty," I say. "We are the Other America he describes in his book. Once again, we are just a number floating in a sea of despair."

"Will his book help you guide your kids?" Mrs. Thompson asks.

"Harrington's book provides a valuable set of tools that I can use to make a difference for my kids. I am teaching my son Richard, who is ten years old, how to budget money—specifically, how to control his spending.

Harrington mentioned that this is not enough. You must give your children hope, encourage them to aspire, and let them know that this will change their lives. All of these elements must be combined to break away from the poverty cycle. Richard is almost ready. When he reaches an age when this will make sense to him, I will pursue it."

"Mary, our conversations reinforce my belief that you are capable of so much more."

I smile. "I do have a difference of opinion with Harrington. While we are financially poor, I do not believe we are impoverished. We have Oriental soul, a cultural pride. We don't suffer incurable diseases, we have clean water, we have shelter, and we believe things can and will get better. If poverty exists in your mind, then we will be emotionally, mentally, or possibly physically impoverished. I don't want my kids to fall into that trap."

"Yes," Mrs. Thompson jumps in, "a recurring theme in Harrington's book is the opposite of what I see in the Japanese culture. The poor in America are almost all undereducated. Japanese culture believes in the importance of education."

"I repeat to my children, 'The greatest economic equalizer is education. This is how you can break the poverty cycle.'"

Over time, these conversations cement our friendship. How odd, as I am sure her husband served as a US naval officer during World War II. Several times as we talk, Mrs. Thompson tears up and says, "Mary, I am so sorry for what you endured and what you lost during the war. It's more than monetary—it was your youth, your pride, and your future opportunities."

The first time I hear her say this, I am silent. Then, after she repeats it several more times, I respectfully respond, "I never look at it as the loss of my future. Yes, I lost what I thought was my future career, and my pride was damaged. In exchange, I gained a family and found my *ikigai*, my purpose in life.

My *ikigai* reinstated much of my pride and brought me joy. I share these feelings with my husband and my kids every day. My future is to be a good wife, a good parent, and a friend to everyone—including you, Mrs. Thompson. I cherish our friendship. It gives me comfort and peace in a world that looks at me differently and treats me accordingly."

Until now, Mrs. Thompson has never heard me speak of the continual mistreatment I received postwar. Her eyes fill with tears as she says, "Mary, we are friends. Thank you."

Many years later, after Mrs. Thompson passes away, I receive a letter from a trustee in California representing Mrs. Thompson's estate. The letter informs me that I am one of her beneficiaries and will receive a monetary gift. Upon receipt, I close my eyes and thank her for being my friend, for looking beyond what she saw, and for taking the time to share her life stories and listen to mine. I am thankful for having known her.

* * *

More hope lifts my spirits on Richard's eleventh birthday, June 10, 1963, when President John F. Kennedy (JFK) gives his famous "A Strategy of Peace" speech. This speech deeply influences me and contributes to molding my philosophies for many years to come.

These words in particular stand out and will always be remembered: "We all inhabit this small planet. We all breathe the same air... and we are all mortal."

He is talking about the Russian people, our longtime enemies of the state. His attempt to humanize them introduces a compassion that opens the door for an agreement between the United States and the Soviet Union to limit the doomsday arms race.

His approach to achieving a balanced humanity through empathy likely saves millions of lives. This action, combined with JFK's introduction of the Civil Rights Act in June 1963, gives me hope for a better life for my children and sparks the roots of my balanced-humanity concept.

In August 1963, this momentum spurs two hundred thousand protestors to march on Washington, DC, in support of this legislation, which is pending in Congress. At the March on Washington another inspirational figure, Dr. Martin Luther King Jr., catches my attention. His "I Have a Dream" speech brings chills to my body and soul, elevating my understanding of his fight for my equality. I have never been so moved by words alone.

Shortly thereafter, on November 22, 1963, a cool Friday afternoon, I am at work cleaning the Meyers' residence in San Marino when news of John F. Kennedy's assassination blares from all televisions and radios within earshot.

I stop working and glare at the television in the den. Newscasters are rapidly spewing comments about the shooting and the installation of Lyndon B. Johnson (LBJ) as our next president. I begin to cry—my loss is not for an unknown president, but for a man who survived the travesties of World War II and was contributing to our social fabric, developing laws to positively address the issues facing me, my family, and many of my World War II camp friends. Unfortunately, before he can complete this work, he meets his fate driving through Dallas, Texas, in a convertible car.

The pictures of Jackie Kennedy's designer clothes dampened with her husband's blood are a cruel sight.

Her eyes are in a constantly dilated state. I, along with the nation, weep for days. In her honor I create an *ikebana* arrangement in which the *shin*, the tallest and most prominent part, is made of a beautiful bird-of-paradise, suggesting her husband's ascension to the spiritual.

John F. Kennedy's work proceeds posthumously with the passing of the Civil Rights Act in 1964, signed into law by President LBJ. This does not stop riots from breaking out in the Watts area of Los Angeles, just fifteen miles from where we live. For six days Los Angeles faces angry crowds surrounded by fires and mayhem.

The cause of the riots centers on racial discrimination and associated poverty. The riots reinforce the need for LBJ's War on Poverty programs, which he mentions in his 1964 State of the Union address. This War on Poverty creates the Office of Economic Opportunity, which spawns programs to advance vocational training, education, financial support to help poor families, and food assistance through food stamps.

Many of the Office of Economic Opportunity policies mirror those contained in Harrington's book *The Other America*. But even with these advances in civil rights, many things remain the same. Activist figures such as Malcolm X emerge to continue the fight for civil rights, but his efforts are cut short when he is assassinated in February 1965.

These events and others that occur before 1967 mark their place in the cultural revolution of the 1960s. The psychedelic music, the excessive experimentation with drugs, free love, and the Vietnam War form the primary ingredients of the decade's legacy. These artifacts and actions are important, but not personal. That changes in 1967 when Set-chan and I test our wedding vows about abandonment.

10

Lessons of Abandonment

In 1967, five years after Set-chan's accident, we are struggling financially, emotionally, and spiritually. Set-chan's disability benefits and my meager earnings from cleaning homes are not enough to live on. We need help to finance Richard's college education and day-to-day expenses.

The afternoon after Richard's graduation from Washington Junior High School in 1967, I sit down next to him at the kitchen table.

"Richard, how do you feel about graduating from Washington Junior High School?"

Richard puts his pen down and looks up from his green spiral notebook, his diary. An English teacher's assignment in ninth grade included keeping a daily diary. Richard loved the assignment and continued writing in his diary after the class ended. He treasures writing. He mentions the elegance of the written word and the rhythms or cadences of spoken language. Although he struggles at it, he loves it. He often writes in his green spiral notebook while sitting quietly outside in the backyard or on the patio.

He smiles and says, "Mom, I love it. Even though I couldn't do all the things I wanted to do, I made some great friends and got to do some fun things. And I have grown eight inches and gained twenty pounds. I'm looking forward to attending John Muir High School."

Focused, I hit him with, "How would you like to live with Uncle Mits?" I am leading up to his summer and possibly beyond.

Richard's forehead wrinkles and he squints his eyes. "What does that mean? What will I be doing?" He frowns and walks away, leaving his pen and diary open on the kitchen table. I am not sure what just happened, but he appears puzzled. Maybe, I was too focused.

I look down at his green spiral notebook and read the first page.

From Richard's journal (no date):

As I have changed, the landscape of the neighborhood has changed over the past three years. The Baptist church across the street, with its majestic gray siding and miraculous steeple, has fallen victim to a terrible fire. In its place, dark ashes and soot form a shifting monument of remembrance. The intense heat generated from the blaze scorched a colorful glaze on my dirty bedroom window, etching a circular pattern of purples and yellows that catch the morning sun. The light turns my window into a kaleidoscope, dispersing the colors throughout my bedroom, reminding me of that once-beautiful church.

The beautiful blue Victorian home that once occupied the adjacent northwestern corner has been torn down to make room for a tilt-up convalescent hospital. Before it was destroyed, a quaint night light on the wraparound porch used to illuminate the night, a beacon of safety and welcome. It has been replaced by a light-box sign that stays on all night, spewing a vicious red-and-black glow—a reminder that across the street, death is waiting.

I love Richard's rich insights into a world that is so new to him—a fifteen-year-old boy who has found his soul at such a young age. Yet, to me, it is not a surprise. I walk down the hallway to Richard's bedroom and knock on the door.

"Come in," he responds.

I open the door to find Richard looking through his Washington yearbook and reading the notes scribbled inside.

He looks up with a contented smile and nods. "Mom, I won the Soroptimist Award and lettered in football, basketball, and track...." His smugness emerges. "It was a great three years."

I pause for a moment. This is the right time to initiate my plan to finance his future education and address our cash problem. I must act now.

"Aunt Kiku and Uncle Mits need help with their nursery in West Los Angeles. Specifically, he needs help with the contract landscaping and the light construction businesses. It will be hard physical work, but honest and well-paying,"

"A summer job would be great. I can use the money for college savings."

"It may be longer. If all works out. Think about it and we can talk tomorrow."

The next evening, Richard, Set-chan, and I are playing cards, a game of rummy, after dinner at the kitchen table. I am visibly agitated and anxious. Richard asks me if anything is wrong.

I clumsily struggle, "Do you have an answer about working for Uncle Mits?"

Set-chan is stoic and silent. I cannot look Richard in the eye and look down instead. I feel guilty, like a child in trouble.

"I like the idea of a summer job. I'm in."

"This may be longer than just the summer.... This may be longer than that."

Richard's tone turns rigid. "For how long?"

"Possibly, long enough to fund your college education."

As those words leave my mouth, Richard's face turns pale. I look into his empty eyes and see both my failure and his loss of hope. I cannot allow him to lose hope.

"Uncle Mits will help you with college expenses," I say quickly. "It is logical and practical. It isn't an adoption, but it may be. Uncle Mits is a good man."

Richard turns his back to Set-chan and me, and then gets up and walks through the living room and down the long hallway to his bedroom. I hear him collapse on his bed. I hesitate, but then I follow the same path and knock on his bedroom door. When I enter, Richard sits up. He isn't crying, frowning, or angry. He looks numb.

"Richard, times are exceedingly difficult. If we can make this work, well, it will take a heavy load off Dad and me."

Richard looks up and takes in my lined face, my pronounced gray hair, and my aged posture. I am only forty-five, but the last five years have aged me twenty. He looks down at my work-worn white shoes and hesitates. Focusing on them, I notice the dark scuff marks—they bring a chill to my spine. These are the same shoes I was wearing when Richard answered my silent screams for help.

He clears his throat. "Mom, I understand," he mumbles. "I have seen our money journals, and I have seen how the stress has taken a toll on you."

Knowing a decision has been made, I smile as I stand in the bedroom doorway. "Let's not delay. Tomorrow morning we can drive to your Uncle Mits's place in West Los Angeles. Please pack what you need tonight."

I quietly watch Richard get up and start sorting things to take with him. In his closet is the family's one gray Samsonite suitcase, scuffed yet sturdy, that we always use when traveling. Richard lays it flat on his twin-size bed and clicks it open. Like a large clamshell, it lies there menacingly, ready to devour his few items of clothing. It takes him only thirty minutes to fill the suitcase and three brown paper grocery bags with clothes and some additional essentials: his green spiral notebook, a few BIC pens, envelopes, stamps, and one book. After watching him pack, I walk to my bedroom and prepare for bed, holding on to the hope that his future path will lead to success.

In the distance, I hear Richard mumble, "I am no longer wanted."

I toss and turn, finding it difficult to sleep. I am haunted by dreams of falling and never reaching solid ground. Occasionally, my dreams find me struggling in a pool of mud, unable to swim, float, or crawl to safety. I dream of an awful drowning and choking that awakens me several times during the night: 2 a.m., 3 a.m., then 5 a.m. Each time I wake feeling helpless, suffocated by a presentiment of failure.

I am up early, ready to drive Richard to Uncle Mits's house. It is already hot and hazy, foreshadowing a tormenting drive without air-conditioning. Tasting sour and bitter food lodged in the back of my throat, I close my eyes, clamp my hand over my mouth, and hold my stomach. My nerves are protesting against the small meal I had for dinner. After combing my hair and putting my false teeth in place, I walk down the hallway to the kitchen and start to prepare breakfast. I rarely eat breakfast, but today will be an exception.

I hear Richard lugging the gray Samsonite suitcase down the hall and through the living room. He makes another trip to and from his bedroom. Holding his three brown paper grocery bags filled with clothes, he stands at the kitchen door. I place two eggs onto his plate, and he sets down the paper bags, sits at the table, and patiently waits for a slice of bacon. Silence accompanies his meal.

Rather than washing the dishes, I leave them in the sink. We need to go now.

Together we walk to the detached garage—I never like to be in it when it is dark inside. The bare crossbeams accentuate the dark shadows cast along the roofline. The crossbeams are larger than most, as Set-chan wanted to reinforce the structure so he could hang his large ladders and heavy tools out of the way. After his accident, all the ladders and tools were sold, and the bare, solid beams have nothing hanging from them except dark memories.

I open the garage door, where I am greeted by the family car, a 1965 Ford Galaxy. I place the key into the trunk lock and open the lid to the massive rear space. We load the suitcase and the brown paper grocery bags into the trunk. I open the front door and momentarily look up, feeling sick to my stomach. I can no longer see the sunlight outside. I begin choking on my own saliva. I swallow and close my eyes, trying to overcome a swirl of emotions, and find a calm within myself.

Sitting quiet and queasy in the front bench seat, I wish we had seat belts installed. It is rumored they will be required in the next few years. The other option I wish we had is air-conditioning. Richard wanted an FM radio, an eight-track tape player, and power windows instead of the flimsy, dark-blue, plastic crank handles. The car reflects our family life: bland, cheap, and practical. Off-white with a light-blue cloth interior, it was bought as a demo—we never buy a new car, as it loses too much of its value as soon as it is driven off the lot

When we arrive at Uncle Mits's home, he greets us with a big smile. "Come in—it's great to see both of you. Let me take the suitcase and paper bags. Let me show you Richard's bedroom."

In the bedroom, I help him settle in. It is large, with small windows, and the scent of fresh paint and carpet fills my nose. Mits had bought a new bed and new furniture, including an oak dresser and a chest with five drawers. Richard dumps the three grocery bags of clothes into the middle and bottom drawers, saving the top drawer for something important and personal. Mits places the Samsonite suitcase onto the bed, and Richard opens the gray clamshell and unpacks its contents.

I stand back and survey the room again; it is sterile and nice. No pictures anywhere, no personal belongings, and no sense of color. The walls are a clean Navajo white, and the carpet is a light beige, with shadows that shift depending on the angle from which it is viewed. It reminds me of a hospital room with carpet.

Mits leaves the room, providing some private time for Richard and me. I sit down next to Richard on his new bed and smile.

"Do you remember the nautilus seashell we saw at Pacific Ocean Park that was from Japan?" I ask. "It had a continuous spiral. You were fascinated by the way the light caught its colors and the array of patterns. Do you remember it?"

Richard closes his eyes. I hope he is recalling the fluorescent shell.

"I remember the sunlight capturing every edge of the spiral seashell," he says.

"Remember how I showed you the patterns were not all unique but, in fact, repeated themselves, over and over?"

"Yes, I remember .... Why did they do that?"

"Richard, just as those patterns repeated themselves on that seashell, there are reoccurring patterns in life. And if you develop the skill to see these patterns, then you can use them to your benefit, to create your future."

I am not sure if Richard understands. "Your experience here will help you develop that skill—the skill to see patterns in life. I know it doesn't seem like it right now, but you will grow from this experience and live a better life. Please, place this in perspective." I pause and give him a gentle smile. "Remember, someday this will all make sense."

Richard looks bewildered. I ramble on. "Growing up on a farm, we understood certain things. We cannot control the forces of nature: wind, rain, storms, or sunshine. We *can* control and take responsibility for our actions: hard work, fairness, integrity, honesty, compassion, sadness, and joy."

Richard sighs and I smile. "Richard, this may be summer, but let it be your spring, a time of new beginnings and new growth. If you do this, during the summer harvest you will reap the many rewards of wisdom gained."

His confused and troubled face saddens me. I leave the room and quickly reappear with scissors and a sheet of white paper. I pick up the scissors and cut the paper with surgical precision. I begin folding the paper, carefully creasing each new fold, until the paper is tightly folded and compressed.

"I am making an origami flower for you to see how this time and experience can bring insight into your future." I unfold the paper and continue talking. "See how life unfolds in front of you." As the last fold of paper is opened, I start to transform the sharp folds into softer radiuses, forming the flower petals. When I am finished, there sits a beautiful, eight-petaled paper flower, reflecting the intricacies of nature and life.

"When you understand this experience, you can then create patterns in your life. You can form your life as this paper is formed—you can create a future that unfolds into the beauty of your dreams, constructed in the way you want to see it and live it."

Sensing his uncertainty, I leave him with a final thought. "Above all else, be flexible and adaptable. Move with the wind. The strongest structures in nature bend with the wind. That's how they survive and thrive. Remember, there are no coincidences in life, just unrecognized patterns."

Richard smiles, but I'm not sure he fully understands. I step forward and hug him.

Mits reappears. "Ready for the tour?"

We both look up and shrug. "Okay."

We follow Uncle Mits as he gives us the tour. He chuckles between each sentence and bounces around the house like a child playing a playground game. He is proud of his new home, which is only three years old. The house is essentially a long tunnel shaped like an army barracks.

"Okay, enough of the tour. You hungry?"

Richard looks up. "Yeah."

Mits leads us into the kitchen and props open the refrigerator door. Facing us is a grocery store display of fresh foods, juices, soda, eggs, and meats. When Richard first sees the inside of the refrigerator, his eyes look like large saucers.

His uncle just laughs. "We eat well here." Mits rubs his belly and laughs some more. Boyishly, he asks, "I'm not sure what you have in your refrigerator at home, but I hope this is okay?"

I am embarrassed to answer.

Wrinkles appear in Mits's forehead, projecting a sense of concern. "If there is anything you like that isn't here . . . just let me know."

I see Richard slowly swallowing to clear the tears that are choking his throat. I quickly respond, "Mits, I have never seen anything like this except in the grocery stores—"

Mits interrupts, asking, "Is there something we need that you have at home in your refrigerator?"

I see his solicitude and know I should answer. What should I say? Should I tell him that everything I could ever imagine is in his refrigerator, or should we ask for something else?

Before another thought runs through my mind, Richard blurts out, "Our refrigerator at home is always...nearly empty...."

Uncle Mits contains his shock with a blank stare. A seldom-used frown appears on his face, and he slowly closes the door to the refrigerator. Richard looks down with tear-soaked eyes and walks away, ashamed of exposing the truth.

In that one moment, Mits sees his damaged nephew. "I will never ask that question again," he mumbles.

I hurry out of the kitchen, through the living room, and out the front door, Mits following behind me.

Mits lowers his head. "Don't worry, Mary, I will take care of him as if he were my son."

I turn around. "Thank you, Mits. Please take care of him for me."

As I walk out to the car and out of Richard's life, my heart sinks. Once inside the car, I sit frozen, my emotions numb. I am leaving Richard behind. He is alone, to be his uncle's son.

* * *

The days that follow are filled with letters from Richard.

First letter from Richard (no date):
There are no longtime friends to talk to and no immediate way to communicate with them. I am afraid to ask Uncle Mits if I may call long distance.

After you left, I slowly walked back to my room, fell onto the bed, and stared at my green spiral notebook. I jotted down my emptiness with spiral tears. We had an early dinner that evening. Tomorrow marks the start of my new working life.

With his slightly cracked, black-rimmed eyeglasses sliding down his wide nose, Mits reminds me of a chubby Japanese American version of Buddy Holly. He constantly repeats, "If anything happens or you get lost, our address on Federal Avenue is . . . " I will never forget my uncle's address.

Letter from Richard (July 1967):

My days in West Los Angeles are long; up at 5 a.m. so we can be at the nursery by 6 a.m. The roach wagon arrives at 7 a.m. I've started eating a regular breakfast, which consists of a breakfast burrito with hash browns. I eat well and I eat a lot.

Uncle Mits may be short in stature, but he is strong. Although his lower back often bothers him, on many occasions I see him picking up large tree barrels, using the strength in his legs and arms. He served in the Army near the end of World War II. It isn't clear what he did, but he is proud to be a veteran.

Another letter from Richard (July 1967):

Mom, I'm still working six days a week, from 6 a.m. to 6 p.m. The landscapers that come into the nursery for supplies have adopted me, or maybe I'm just some sort of mascot. Their stories of great mansions in Bel Air and Beverly Hills leave me awestruck. I am working with a good friend of Uncle Mits, Bob, installing landscaping at Zsa Zsa Gabor's house. Or maybe Bob is kidding me; I never met or saw her, so I am not sure if it is really her house.

We have built elaborate ponds for movie stars. Most have been truly kind, but others—the beautiful people, as some call them—have punished and looked down on me for being poor. Not having the advantage of money or an exceptional appearance or a great lineage, I fall into the background, and I am mostly invisible in this world.

The work has produced some muscles that help me stand upright and proud. I put on five pounds. Tanned, healthy, and very alive, I look like Southern California suits me. At night in the darkness of my room, while trying to fall asleep, I pick up the origami flower you made that first day and am reminded of your days on the chicken farm in Gardena. I have gained an appreciation for your early working life.

I miss home. I miss Pasadena. I miss my friends. I miss you guys, Mom and Dad. I miss the evening sunsets from across the Rose Bowl. I miss everything that was safe and secure. I even miss the drone of the police helicopters at night, with their spotlights illuminating our yard. I miss all things familiar.

There are many nights when I am too tired to talk to my uncle and aunt, too tired to watch television, and too tired to be in pain. Yet, having cried myself to sleep, in the middle of every night I wake, alone

*in the dark, with only my origami flower to keep me
company.*

Letter from Richard (August 1967):
*The end of August marks two months since I left
home in Pasadena. Uncle Mits and I went to see
University High School. He wants to talk to you
about enrolling me there.*

*Pasadena is my comfort. West Los Angeles is like
a foreign country to me. The early-morning fog,
the critical movie stars, and the absence of longtime friends makes me yearn for home. I'm not sure
where I belong. How can I find my new identity
when the old one is lost? I just want to come home.*

After reading his many letters, I cannot hide from the
truth: I have abandoned him. I have done what my parents
did to me and what Set-chan's father did to him. How did
this happen? Poverty has many voices and fears. Mine was
the fear that we would be unable to feed and educate my
mystical son. At fifteen years of age, Richard just wants to
come home.

* * *

It is a hot and sticky weekend in September 1967. Mits drives
Richard from West Los Angeles to our home in Pasadena to
pick up his remaining clothes and things. Upon their arrival,
we talk; parent to child, and sometimes adult to adult. Mits
steps outside to get some air.

In our kitchen, sitting around the green metal-flake kitchen table that seats ten, Richard begs Set-chan and me to let him come home.

"I want to come home," he pleads.

I shrink into a corner of the room.

"I want to come home . . . . Why can't I come home?"

A tear is forming in the bottom of my right eye, and I stop it from falling. Richard is begging to come home. It comes down to money.

I step out of the corner. "We don't have enough money to keep you here . . . ." My heart drops. This is the first time I have admitted it. "We don't have enough money to keep you here." I don't know what else to say. It is true. "Our cash is running low, and we have very little coming in." I continue to drive this home—we are running out of cash. "We live in a world run by money. To survive, you must have cash. After Daddy's accident, we had very little in savings. The insurance settlement for the accident was small, and it is our only emergency fund."

Richard's face is contorted, projecting perplexity. "I know you told me it was small, but how can the compensation for crippling Dad amount to such a small sum? How can the damages for a person running into a parked car, without provocation, and pinning two people between two parked cars for hours, be so small? How can this happen? How can Dad's life be so meaningless and worthless?"

When he learns the amount of the insurance settlement, Richard becomes visibly angry.

We revisit the family expenses: how much money the family has in savings, our ongoing expenses, and the large medical bills, which will not be reimbursed

"Mom, I know I can do this....I know I can work full-time and cover my living expenses."

As he utters these words, I see terror in his eyes. I sit on the green vinyl kitchen chair at the head of the table. It is noticeably more worn than the other chairs. The curled ridge around the seat cushion is ripped and worn through. Set-chan always complains that the kids are too rough on the furniture. He never points out the extraordinary wear on this vinyl kitchen chair. He insists that it be kept at the head of the kitchen table for him—he never complains that it is the most tattered. I feel uneasy sitting on it.

There is a long pause in our conversation. I see our predicament, but I am perplexed, unable to find a solution. My eyes roll upward as I picture a three-year-old ghost. I think back to when I was adopted by my aunt and uncle. Set-chan has retreated into silence. Is he reminded that he never knew his parents? That from the age of four, he was raised in Hiroshima by his grandmother, halfway around the world from his father?

"We miss you, Richard," I say.

Richard stands in front of me, staring intensely into my eyes. I see his pain. I see and sense the weight of his loneliness. I know that whatever our final decision, he will obey. Set-chan shows no emotion, yet beneath the surface, like an iceberg, the vast majority of him is scared. I am afraid of losing my mystical son. I am afraid of losing what I know about him. I am afraid that a voice of loneliness will join forces with a voice of poverty to hold Richard captive forever. I am afraid of failing my *ikigai*. Then Set-chan smiles, and I now know the right answer.

I reopen the conversation. "We have always told you to assimilate into society; this is the Japanese way, to quietly assimilate into society. Our hope was that you would do this at Mits's place. Our hope was that you could find yourself and integrate, rather than separate yourself from the kids in West Los Angeles."

I shrug, hoping that a combined humanity is workable and possible. I see peace in Richard's eyes, and I look down, feeling a sudden calm that infuses my next words with gentleness.

"Okay," I say softly.

Set-chan and I have learned the lesson of our own abandonment. In September of 1967, it is decided Richard should come home.

* * *

In the heat of a West Los Angeles Indian summer, I pick up Richard in our familiar white Ford Galaxy. He greets me at the front door of Mits's house, ready to come home. Behind him is one packed gray Samsonite suitcase and the three original brown paper grocery bags stuffed with his clothes. Behind his belongings stands Mits.

"Richard, please load the car with your belongings," I say. "I need a moment to chat with Mits."

There is more to Mits than what he appears to be. Many see him as a common laborer, a landscaper managing a nursery. He seldom talks about his brother, who is a medical doctor. He never complains that he was expected to run his father's nursery. He never complains that his life is what it is instead of what he wanted it to be. His actions have always been thoughtful and precise, and he possesses a mind that is unchallenged and clearly capable. I see his genius and his desire for knowledge.

Mits stands quietly in front of me while I collect my thoughts. "Mits, thank you for taking such good care of Richard. He told me you taught him how to drive a truck with a compound low gear, shared your military stories, and allowed him to feed your pet ground squirrel. Most of all, I want to thank you for showing him kindness."

After our conversation, he extends his right hand. "Thank you, Mary." With a quick lift of his brows, he smiles. His childlike mannerisms are comforting and comical. I smile back, understanding that this period of personal growth and direction are now a part of Richard. I shake his hand, feeling his sadness, and know that Richard will never forget him.

Once outside, I absorb the heat of an Indian summer. The light fragrance of autumn is in the air. The morning is aging quickly, and it is time to go. The sun is bright and glowing, spewing radiant heat onto everything in its path.

We step into our car, and I roll down my window and look at Mits's new house, the manicured front lawn, and his tormented smile. I start the car, shift into drive, and slowly pull away from the curb. The painful suffering of my childhood experience has stopped me from repeating history. Our drive is taken with my eyes wide open and my heart the same. No words are spoken. Sighs of relief from both Richard and me signal our passage home. We are both safe.

Upon arriving home, I say, "Richard, you have sensitivity. Yes, you have a rational side, but you have sensitivity, and because of this you understand humanity—never forget that."

Richard looks up. His voice finally breaks the silence. "I will never forget."

Richard writes his thoughts about his return home in his notebook.

From Richard's journal (no date):
I have returned to the comfort of my home in Pasadena. I don't miss the newness of my uncle's home, the nice furniture, the full refrigerator, or the safe neighborhood. None of that matters, because I got to come home and be with Dad, Mom, my brother, and my friends. This is what is important to me. This is what I've learned: What is important to me is finding home, being surrounded by family and people you really know. Love generates an energy that percolates from within.

With help from my parents, I have landed a full-time job at a friend's gas station. I work every day after school from 3:30 to 9:30 p.m., all day on Saturday, and a half day on Sunday. The owners, Yoji and Ernie Arai, are from Hiroshima and are both survivors of the atomic bomb. They pay me minimum wage, $1.50 per hour. I am ecstatic. I like the work uniforms; they are blue, crisp, and say "Atlantic Richfield."

At the gas station I work with a grumpy Black mechanic, Tracy. He is partially shaven and often smells of Brown's BBQ ribs, as I do. Brown's BBQ Ribs is located across the street from the gas station. Our favorite paper-plate special is a set of three

BBQ ribs, cornbread, and beans. Add a Dr. Pepper and Tracy and I are in heaven.

The Christmas of 1967 is my true homecoming. A bit of money in my pocket meant I could and did buy our family a five-foot Christmas tree, lights, some new ornaments, and two boxes of tinsel. The scent of the tree, the glimmering lights, and the gas heater in the fireplace removes the damp chill in the air. No matter how poor we might be, Christmas is and will always be important to me. It is a time of giving, sharing, and hoping for the world to be a better place. For me it is a time to forget the tragedy that I may face tomorrow. It is a time of spirit and joy. I love Christmas.

A few years later, he adds this entry.

From Richard's journal (no date):
On December 29, four days after Christmas and one day before his sixtieth birthday, Uncle Mits passes away. The causes of death are recorded as acute myocardial infarction, atherosclerotic heart disease, and diabetes mellitus. He was a great man. I will never forget him. Mits, Mom, and Dad saved me. Economic poverty can hurt you, but emotional poverty will destroy you.

Richard shares these passages in his journal with me many years later, reinforcing my belief that he will never forget the summer of 1967. I, too, will never forget that summer. During the winter of 1967, I became comfortable with Richard's return home and the world around us. That would soon change.

11

An Oriental Boy
in America

The country is rocked by war and violent storms of racial turbulence that affect our family. In April 1968, a year after Richard's return home, while sitting in the living room watching the evening news on television, I am held captive by these words from Walter Cronkite: "Dr. Martin Luther King, the apostle of nonviolence in the civil rights movement, has been shot to death in Memphis, Tennessee."

I get up from the couch and shuffle to the den. Isolated and alone, I sit quietly crying for the loss of someone who cared about us, the Other Americans. I cry for the death of his effort to be heard declaring the need for equality. Why would anybody kill the recipient of a Nobel Peace Prize?

Striking closer to home, on Wednesday, five days before Richard's sixteenth birthday in 1968, Walter Cronkite announces on television, "Polls indicate Robert F. Kennedy is solidly leading in the Democratic vote." This brings joy to my heart, as his brother did so much to fight for our civil rights. I go to bed, hopeful for more progress.

Thursday morning is beautiful. When I arrive at the Powells' to clean their home, the Mister and Misses are glued to the television. I hear echoing throughout the house, "Robert F. Kennedy was assassinated in the Ambassador Hotel in downtown Los Angeles last night."

Later that evening, sitting at the kitchen table after dinner, Richard and I talk about these events.

"We talked about the assassination in school today," Richard says. "The person they arrested lived next door to a friend of mine here in Pasadena. The killer went to John Muir High School. I can't believe someone who attended my high school killed Robert F. Kennedy. Why?"

"I don't know why. It's a terrible act," I mutter.

Richard says, "Between these killings and the draft for the Vietnam War, I'm just not sure how we got here. Older school friends are coming back from the war totally out of it. I can't talk to them anymore. And the ones I do talk to are so spacey, they're not who I remember. Sometimes they check out of the conversation, and minutes of silence go by before they return. What's wrong with these guys?"

"I don't know. I do know that war is terrible for everyone, soldiers and civilians. By the way, did you say someone who went to your high school was the assassin?" I ask.

"Yes, I was told his name is Sirhan Sirhan." After Richard's response, he quickly returns to the war. "Mom, the draft has collected many of my older friends for military duty. One of my friend's moms told me, 'This meritless war has spread my son's ashes and emotional remains over our family.' Why are we fighting these people?"

The next day I get a firsthand glimpse into this emotional carnage. A few of Richard's veteran friends come over to visit. I find them polite, but vacant. The older brother of one of Richard's close friends is a former Army sergeant. He stands in our kitchen while I am cooking, and I ask him about his military experience in Vietnam. Avoiding eye contact, he looks down at his feet and mumbles, "The GI Bill has been great. It covered my college expenses."

After he leaves our house, Richard mentions, "Mom, none of these guys who have served in-country talk about it. They don't want people to know they are Vietnam vets. They have been spat on, called names, and badgered."

I am shocked. Men who have fought a war on behalf of our country are treated like lepers—why? I flash back to my high school friends, Mrs. Ichino's husband, and Uncle Roy, who were members of the 442nd in World War II. Were they treated poorly?

* * *

In the late spring of 1970 Richard's focus shifts to high school graduation and the events surrounding it. Richard has a crush on a white girl. He often tries to hide that he is talking to her on the telephone, but mothers know these things. A few weeks before his senior prom, I am sitting in the living

Richard in his high school letterman jacket

room, watching television. Richard is in the kitchen on the telephone. I hear him grunt; then there is a loud thud as he slams our telephone handset onto the hard plastic cradle.

I get up and enter the kitchen. "Richard, please stop being so rough on things."

And then, life explodes. Richard screams, "You may be an American citizen, but you will never be an American and you will never date my daughter." His words echo repeatedly in my ears. He storms out of the kitchen and stomps down the hall to his bedroom, yelling, "I am invisible. Why am I an outcast of society?"

Richard passes Set-chan in the hallway and shouts, "I am the all-American boy. I lettered in sports, I love my beat-up Ford with its four-on-the-floor Hurst shifter and V-8 engine, and I love wearing my letterman's jacket when I ride my motorcycle. I hate my Japanese heritage and how I look.

"I want to be blond and blue-eyed. I want to have white skin. I want to be English, or Scottish, or maybe French or German. But no, I am an Oriental, a Japanese American who clearly looks inferior to a white person. No matter which way I turn, my reflection is the same—I look Japanese. There is no mistaking that, and there is nowhere I can hide from it."

Set-chan stands in the hallway, shaken and dejected. Richard turns his back on him, shunning him, and continues storming down the hallway to his room.

I stand paralyzed in the kitchen. I quickly regain my composure and walk through the living room and down the hallway. When I reach his room, Richard slams the door in my face and screams as loud as he can, releasing a storm of anger and frustration. I hear him hurl his fist into the solid closet door, creating a reverberating echo throughout the house.

"I hate myself," Richard screams. Then another outburst, a desperate cry for help. "I don't belong here."

He rambles on, "I hate my parents. How dare they bring me into a world where I am constantly ridiculed? How dare they do this to me? There is no excuse for this. The more I see my reflection, the greater my anger. I hate what I look like. I hate who I am."

His screams of anguish project beyond the walls of the house. Without knocking, I swing open the door. My pulse is racing, but I stop, take a deep breath, and try to speak thoughtfully.

"You will never escape what you look like," I say. "I understand this. But someday you will be thankful that a part of you is Japanese, and you will never lose that part of yourself."

Richard scoffs dismissively at this. "I see no benefit in being Japanese American," he shouts. "I see no benefit in looking Japanese. I see no benefit in retaining any part of being Japanese."

Set-chan appears at Richard's bedroom door and, in a low, cracking voice, says, "When you walk away from the last piece of sushi on the plate, remember, you did not take it because you are not hungry. You did not take it because of your Japanese pride and etiquette, *enryo*."

He slowly and deliberately repeats, "You did not take the last piece of sushi because a big part of you is still Japanese. . . . Remember that."

Stunned, Richard looks up, frowns, then looks down and says, "I hate him for knowing this. I hate him for being right." He slams his fist into the closet door mirror, shattering it into tiny bits of sparkling glass while shouting, "I cannot ignore all the mirrors in the world, nor can I ignore the deep cultural roots of being Japanese American."

Dripping blood on the bedroom floor, he screams, "Dad is wrong." Tears falling and nose running uncontrollably, he sits down on his bed, bends over, rests his head in his bloodied hands, and cries out, "Mom, you are wrong. I hate not being able to change the reflections in the mirror, or the reflections in the minds of those around me who ignore me or hate me."

I flash back to my reflection in the train window in 1942, when I was being transported to the Relocation Assembly Center in Tulare, California. Why has nothing changed?

Richard stands up and screams, "I hate myself." He sprays spit and tears onto my face—abusing his rights as my son.

I stand there and shakily say, "You will always be my son, but you are a Japanese American boy . . . a visual immigrant in the eyes of America. They call you Oriental. Use this to become stronger and wiser. Do not be confused—you are an American. Never give up . . . . Never quit." Time stood still.

Breaking the trance, I scurry off to my bedroom and immediately reach for a tissue to wipe off his spit. I flash on my high school years, when Harry, a white varsity football player, had a crush on me. He asked me out many times, and many times I said, "No." Like Richard, I was proud to have my coveted "G" patch, which boasted that I was a Gardena Letter Girl in high school sports.

When I look into my dresser mirror, I see a middle-aged Jap girl. I do not look away. I am no longer haunted by my reflected image. I now realize that Richard and I must become the mirror and show America what we see and what it has refused to see about itself. We are not the enemy. We are Americans.

Part Three

Ikigai—Dreams Live Forever

In Part Two, I related how I learned that my *ikigai* does not comprise grand achievements but is formed by consistent actions rooted in Bushido philosophies, which I share with my children. These final chapters paint the landscape upon which my legacy is passed on to Richard. He saved me in a dark moment, and someday, when it is my time to let go, he will be there again. My death is inevitable. Do not shed tears for me, as this is not a story about dying. This is a story about how dreams and *ikigai* can and should outlive the physical body that once cradled them. *Ikigai*, if properly passed on, lives forever through everyone's dreams.

12

Northern Lights

Ensure your dreams and goals extend beyond your life-time, and you will never be lost or without purpose and joy—this is your *ikigai*. I tell this to Richard many times, and many times I remind him that he is a major part of my life's purpose, my *ikigai*. Richard shares his dreams, his frustrations, his fears, his joys, and his goals with me through letters, telephone calls, journals, and face-to-face conversations.

One year after the devastating confrontation in which Richard declared his hatred of being Japanese American, in the early-morning hours of February 9, 1971, we experience a structurally damaging earthquake. Aftershocks rumble into the afternoon while Richard attends classes at Pasadena City College (PCC).

The evening after that devastating earthquake, Richard walks in the back door two hours earlier than normal. His typical shift working at the Showcase liquor store on North Lake Avenue ends at midnight. The owner, Bob Breault, is a sound engineer for Columbia Records who is known for his role in the first Santana album. Randomly, he asks Richard to bring various alcoholic beverages to him when he is recording at the CBS sound studios located at Sunset and Gower. Richard loves hanging out with the musicians and vocalists. Tonight, something is different. His complexion is pale; could he be catching a cold? After he locks the back door behind him, he sits down at the kitchen table, trembling uncontrollably. Silence separates us.

"No invite to Shelly's Manne-Hole tonight?" I am kidding, as he is never invited.

He looks up, still shaking, and stutters, "Mom, we were robbed tonight…at gunpoint. There were three of them…. Each had a gun pointed at me, Chris, and our night manager, Darrel." Richard gets up from the kitchen table, slowly walks through the living room and down the hall to his bedroom, and gently closes the door.

In shock, I instinctively follow him and stand outside his door, wanting to enter and console him. The lights in his bedroom flick off, and I hear him plop onto his bed. Best to let him rest.

The next morning, we meet at the kitchen table. Richard's face is still pasty, as if soaked in Ivory soap.

"I looked through the police mug books last night," he says, his speech slurred, "and several of my friends from high school are in them."

"Did you recognize the robbers?" I ask.

"No." He stops and looks up. "Mom, I can't sing, I can't dance, I'm not handsome, I don't have wealth or rich parents, I don't have exceptional athletic skills, and I am not brilliant or exceptionally smart. I think it's time for me to leave

Southern California." Getting up from the table, Richard smiles. "Mom, maybe it's just time."

* * *

In the summer of 1971, Richard receives an invitation to stay with a friend in White Plains, New York. After his visit, the friend asks Richard to drive cross-country with him, but Richard is reluctant to spend any portion of his college fund, which he has been diligently saving over the past four years. He approaches me to ask for advice. I know I should encourage him to take advantage of the invitation.

"Richard, have you ever been outside of California?"

Richard smiles. "No, Mom, and you know that."

I say, "Well, it's about time." I stand up and place my hands on my hips.

Richard says, "Isn't this a foolish use of my college savings?"

"This is part of your education," I snap back. "Don't lose this opportunity. Sometimes opportunities arise that are not part of the original plan. Don't give up the plan, but don't miss out on living life either."

Richard smiles and nods. "True, Mom. I missed Woodstock two years ago."

I sit back down and mumble, "In many ways, I am glad you missed it."

* * *

Before Richard can leave for New York, however, there is one major event hanging over him. His future could be derailed by the Vietnam War military draft. On August 5, 1971, the draft lottery, which will determine which men born in 1952 will be drafted into military service, is televised. Birth dates are randomly chosen and assigned numbers corresponding to the order in which men will be drafted. I pray that this opportunity passes him by. I do not want my son to fight in a war halfway around the world.

As birthdays are selected, I anxiously watch our television from the comfort of my living room couch. The first hundred birthdays are announced, and then the second hundred. It is not until number 226 that Richard's birthday is picked. His draft number is far beyond the highest number to be drafted. My son will not be going to war. He can now take his cross-country trip without anxiety, and his college career is now on track with his timetable. I sit back, feeling blessed.

Ten days later he flies to New York. On the drive home he writes letters to me every day. This letter outlines his impression of San Jose:

Letter from Richard (August 1971):

Hi Mom,

Ken and I should be home in three days. This letter may arrive after I return, but I want to share with you what I experienced in San Jose. We exited Highway 101 onto Santa Clara Street. In the middle of downtown San Jose is the college, San Jose State. The old buildings welcomed me. On campus, I sat on the lawn facing one of the brick dorms—Royce Hall. I closed my eyes and sensed a peace. I belong here, Mom, and I will return.

Richard's letter continues:

I spent one hour at the library on campus. A librarian gave me a brochure about the school. San Jose

State is the oldest public school of higher education in California. It was founded in 1857. California became a state in 1850 two years after the California Gold Rush officially ended. It will be a fresh start for me. Ironic that the next California boom will again start in Northern California. This time it will be silicon, not gold, that will fuel endless dreams and change my life.

When Richard returns home from the New York trip, he is constantly smiling, and I see hope in his eyes.

Richard's green journal sits on the kitchen table, begging to be read. He has reminded me many times that it is okay if I read it—we have no secrets. I am curious about his thoughts and worry about him venturing to Northern California on his own. Before breakfast on the morning of Richard's departure to San Jose, February 2, 1972, I muster the courage to read his journal.

From Richard's journal (no date):
On December 23, 1971, bundled with another stack of incoming Christmas cards, my acceptance notice for the 1972 spring term at San Jose State arrives. It is my Christmas present; my special wish to Santa Claus has been granted. I eagerly open the starched white envelope and unfold the letter inside, preserving every original crease and edge. For one hour I stare at the letter. I fold it, then unfold it.

From Richard's journal (Friday, December 31, 1971):

New Year's Eve on Colorado Boulevard in Pasadena plays witness to thousands of people camping on street sidewalks. Three of my high school friends and I ride our motorcycles till dawn, waving to friends and out-of-town visitors. We wish everyone a happy New Year and welcome them to a great tradition—the Pasadena Rose Parade. These moments shared with friends and strangers make Pasadena the special place I call home.

From Richard's journal (Tuesday, February 1, 1972):

I survey my belongings. I will take everything except my jet-black 1966 Honda Scrambler 250cc motorcycle. I can think of only one person who could take it, care for it, and make it run forever. That is John Idoni. We have known each other since we were seven years old. We met shortly after John arrived from Italy. He became a fixture in our predominantly Black neighborhood in Pasadena. Ironically, John once admitted it wasn't until many years later that he realized he wasn't Black.

I place his journal down and walk through the house. Finding myself at his bedroom door, I knock three times.

"Good morning, Richard, isn't it time to get up?" My voice reverberates through the hollow bedroom door. I glance at my watch to verify it is 6 a.m.

"Yeah, Mom . . . thanks. I'll be up in just a minute."

My tone is firm. "Remember, it's important that you eat breakfast today. You have a long drive ahead of you, and if I don't feed you this morning and something happens to—"

Richard abruptly cuts me off. "Okay, okay... I'm up."

"Okay, breakfast is ready. I want you to eat it before it gets cold."

As I quickly shuffle down the long hallway to the living room, I hear Richard mumbling something incomprehensible, and I think, *He's not getting up.*

In the kitchen, I place the plate holding two eggs, sunny-side up, and two bacon strips in the oven to keep warm. Sitting at the kitchen table, my mind keeps rolling through Richard's numbers.

"Mom." Richard's voice breaks my train of thought.

"Yes," I quickly respond. "We are proud of you, son. I wish that I could go with you and help you move into the dorms, like we did with your older brother at Cal. But I know you will be fine on your own."

Richard's face is a mix of emotions; his eyes are sad and his forehead wrinkled, but he is smiling.

"It's important I tell you about my older sister, your Aunt Shizuye." Richard doesn't know much about his Aunt Shizuye, as she spoke limited English and kept to herself. I take a deep breath. "Your Aunt Shizuye, her husband, Shigeji, and their four children lived in Manchuria from the mid-1930s to the mid-1940s—"

Richard interrupts. "Mom, I didn't know I had two more cousins."

"Let me finish. The four children were born close together in 1938, 1940, 1942, and 1944. Shigeji was a manager in a very big Japanese company, Mantetsu—the South

Manchuria Railway Company, Ltd. Shigeji was a good manager who developed strong working and personal relationships with his Chinese coworkers."

Richard, mesmerized, asks, "Mom, how do you know so much about this?"

"I will explain later—back to the story before I forget parts of it. During this time Japan encouraged its citizens to immigrate to Northern China. When war was declared between the United States and Japan, things in China rapidly deteriorated. It was no longer safe for Japanese workers in China. Because your Aunt Shizuye and Uncle Shigeji had been kind and humane to the Chinese workers, they protected them during the war years. In 1945, after the Japanese surrendered, the Chinese railway workers helped your Aunt Shizuye and your cousins get out of China and back to Japan. Unfortunately, the two younger children, Makoto and Hiroko—ages one and three—faced with treacherous travel conditions, lack of clean water and food, and physical stress, died from malnutrition."

Richard looks puzzled. "Mom, what does this have to do with me going away to college?"

I clear my throat again and whisper, "Richard, you will meet many new people at school. Please respect each one and treat them accordingly, for your survival may depend upon it."

Richard nods. "I understand."

After breakfast, Richard smiles to see his life packed in a green army duffle bag and a few paper shopping bags. This day is his bridge to a better life. "Education is the greatest economic equalizer," I have told him many times, while adding in many other nuggets of hope and inspiration.

How ironic that now, thirty years after I packed up to leave home, my son is doing the same. But this time, unlike me, he will gain his freedom and independence. I thank God for that.

My last words before his departure are: "You must look beyond what you cannot see; then you must go beyond what you first thought impossible."

As Richard drives away, I yearn for his return.

* * *

The next few years are a blur. Richard is home from school for the summer of 1973. This marks the last time I will spend an extended period with him. He splits the summer between working in an East Los Angeles liquor store and attending the summer session at California State University in Los Angeles.

Walking toward Richard's bedroom, I begin formulating my advice to him about his graduation. I recollect an experience in 1969, when I reconnected with my high school best friend, Mary Uyeda, and we decided to see Spencer Tracy's last movie, *Guess Who's Coming to Dinner*.

Mary (Uyeda) Maruyama and Tome reunited

Accompanying Tracy through this controversial story are Sidney Poitier and his long-time friend, Katharine Hepburn. Poitier, who portrays a Black medical doctor, Dr. Prentice, is planning to marry Houghton's character, who is white, pending the blessing of her parents, portrayed by Tracy and Hepburn. I remind myself that in 1967 the Supreme Court ruled that laws banning interracial marriage were unconstitutional. Dr. Prentice is highly accomplished and has made many contributions to society. His life is beyond reproach. This leaves Tracy's and Hepburn's characters to face only one concern: race.

Tracy knew this would be an important movie and wanted to finish it, regardless of his ailing health. He became a messenger who helped me better understand specific details of my *ikigai*. A few weeks after he completed filming the movie, Tracy passed away on Richard's birthday, June 10, 1967.

Arriving at Richard's bedroom door, I find him quietly reading a textbook. The bedroom walls are littered with pink paint chips and cracks that have grown longer and wider. I knock on the partially open door and enter the room. Richard looks up and smiles.

I immediately start into my message. "Richard, this will be your last year in college. Make it a great year."

Catching his glance, I continue, "I have watched you mature so much these past few years. I have seen what being up north has done for you. Your thoughts, your dreams, and your growth have exceeded anything I could have imagined."

I swallow and catch my breath. "I don't want you to be another Jap boy from a bad neighborhood in Los Angeles, lost and left behind. I don't want you to suffer the indignities and prejudice that I have faced. It is my hope, my *ikigai*, that you will live a better and more dignified life than me. The movie *Guess Who's Coming to Dinner* opened my eyes to how to better prepare you. You must achieve accomplishments and contribute to others. This will position you beyond reproach."

I pause, again catching my breath, before continuing, "Your accomplishments must speak for you. Make them stand out, or no one will listen to you, no one will care, no one will respect you, including yourself, and you will not assimilate into America. You must contribute to both yourself and society. Being Japanese American, you have no social capital to barter. You must continue this cycle of accomplishments and contributions over your entire lifetime."

I hesitate for a moment, afraid of what I am about to say next, knowing there will be no turning back. "Please, make Northern California your new home—do not come back except to visit. Go beyond the small minds here that have tried to hold you back and oppress you, have told you that you are not good enough. Avoid those who belittled you for not attending the right schools or wearing the right clothes, who demeaned you because of your appearance. You must not fall victim again to this vicious pack of cruel people. Do not seek revenge, do not hate them, do not be bitter. Instead, live a better life. No, live a much better life."

Richard sits quietly, waiting for me to finish.

Acknowledging his patience, I continue, "Many people complain about the injustices of our world. Remember, America has given us countless opportunities. My parents came to America to build a better life. Dad and I have talked to you about the American dream. The American dream is still alive—we believe in it. This is what we have prepared you to do and what we want you to achieve. It is up to you to attain it.

"Ask yourself, 'What can be?' or 'What if?' Don't limit yourself to 'what is,' and your mind will remain open and alive."

I take a deep breath. "We are ordinary people, but it is what we do with ourselves that can make life exceptional."

As I nod my head, bow to Richard, and back out of his room, he smiles, acknowledging this moment with silence and respect. I see his energy colliding with opportunities, bursting into bright rays of hope. I dream of future societal norms that enable him to be accepted without compromise—a balanced humanity, an authentic reciprocity of respect and friendship. This is what I wish for my son. When I tell Richard not to come back, I lose a part of my heart. I hope he will take that part of me with him. When summer ends, when he is standing by his car parked in the driveway, when he jumps in and waves goodbye, and when he drives off, I understand this is no longer his home.

13

Gambari

The arrival of a new year, 1974, is marked by Richard's focus on finding a job postgraduation. We have several difficult and tense phone calls in the spring of 1974.

During one of these calls, Richard's voice is tired and whiny, and he drags out his words. "I have mailed hundreds of resumes and letters to prospective employers. I have attended all the on-campus interviews I can. I have responded to employment opportunities posted in the San Jose Unemployment Office. All this search has produced is a stack of rejection letters, which I am burning—yes, burning—tonight. The economy is terrible, the job market is terrible, and I am Japanese American. I am invisible, Mom."

These are excuses, and I will not accept them. My voice reflects my anger and the depth of my care. "If you quit, you will only disappoint me and yourself. You will become emotionally impoverished because you did not try your hardest. You have no *gambari*."

Richard immediately jumps in. "I do have *gambari*. I do have tenacity. I am trying my best. I have *gambari*. I am the year of the dragon—I will persevere." He shouts into the telephone, "I won't quit."

Several days later, on an overcast day in May, we speak again. "Richard, there are no coincidences in life, just unrecognized patterns. Everything happens for a reason," I tell him. "There is a reason the job market is so difficult now, just when you are graduating. Study this pattern and anticipate the next pattern, and you will find your success."

My words fall on deaf ears. Richard is exhausted and does not see the light at the end of the tunnel. Feeling defeated and unable to construct a future for himself, he has quit. He is ashamed.

"Find your strength in these times of despair," I say. "Continue to be kind, compassionate, and empathetic. You will find that by giving during this time, you will receive."

Then something I say, which at first glance seems counterintuitive, seems to make a lot of sense to Richard. "In school you have been taught to find answers using logical formulas or processes. I understand this—I was taught the same. But, in real life, things don't always work that way. Life is chaotic and messy. You must design your life, live it, hope that it falls into place. And if it doesn't, you must adapt and move forward. Life is not linear, but convoluted and holistic. Life is not contrived, but aesthetic and natural."

His receptive silence prompts another story from me. "I remember trying to catch a chicken on the farm so I could chop off its head and pluck its feathers. I would chase one chicken and then another, to no avail. I became frustrated and angry. Why was I so slow? Why did the chickens run from me? How could I do this? Father Kawakita heard the ruckus and came outside and watched me.

"After I had made many attempts, he said, 'Tome, stop. Take a deep breath, clear your mind, and close your eyes. Do not challenge them by running after them. Instead, be still and drop the chicken feed you have been carrying onto the ground. Make them feel comfortable in their world and with their fate. To win this battle, as in all of life, you must affirm that the outcome you desire has already happened.'

"The world around me settled down. I felt one chicken pecking at my feet, and then another, and then another. I opened my eyes, surrounded by chickens calmly sitting next to me. I gently picked up one chicken, without disrupting the others, and walked to the chopping block. I looked straight into the eyes of the chicken and without hesitation, I chopped off its head."

I take a short breath before starting again. "Life seldom follows a straight line. You must accept and embrace the world as it moves within and around you. Richard, quit chasing the chickens."

I laugh and Richard begins laughing with me.

"Mom, my arguments seem silly now," he says. "Your story demonstrates that I should follow a deeper structure within my mind. I am relieved and hopeful."

After a few more difficult phone calls, Richard no longer complains about the poor economy, the terrible job market, and being Japanese American. He does not give up. Instead, he moves forward. He keeps going, hoping that someone will hear him, hire him, or just return the kindness he projects.

Then, a letter from Richard arrives.

Letter from Richard (May 31, 1974):

Hi Mom,

Yesterday, I stepped outside of my apartment on 6th Street and inhaled the coming humid summer heat. I exhaled slowly and felt a summer rain approaching. I trudged along San Salvador Street to campus, catching glimpses of familiar memories along the way.

Passing the brick dorms, I paused and gazed at my original home on campus, Royce Hall. I sadly waved goodbye. My immediate destination was the tall, cube-like building one block away—the business towers. In these concrete pillars are the offices for the professors, the deans, and the administration that make the business school come alive. I needed to drop off a letter, a final act of worship to seal the completion of my studies.

Sitting on the west steps of the business tower, I studied the student union across the concrete path. I remember the first time I felt its mammoth presence. The chairs inside are blockish and uncomfortable. The carpet pattern jumps out at you, a nauseating swirl of dark red, brown, and black. Beer-soaked corners are evidence of late nights with friends and a reminder that no alcohol is allowed. The student union was a gathering place when the smallness of our dorm rooms or apartments closed in on us.

This has been my home for the past two years. Leaving means another loss of family and another adventure alone. I am twenty-one years old and not coming back to Southern California. I promised you I would not return. I promised I would grow beyond the small minds there and find my future here in Silicon Valley.

I will never give up my dreams.

This, the last day of May 1974, is my best friend Russ Fisher's birthday. I looked up, rain began to fall, and clouds puffed into tall pillars of gray anger. The world swirled around me, spreading its arms to unleash relentless gusts of wind. I stood silent and still, opened my eyes, and slowly bent over to gently pick up the chicken.

I have accepted a job offer from a Palo Alto Technology Company. I start next Monday, on my twenty-second birthday.

After reading this letter, I feel a sense of accomplishment and relief. Another lesson learned. I can't wait to follow Richard's new adventures.

14

Discovering Silicon Valley

In high school I wrote and read a lot. I was a journalist on the staff of our school paper, *The Lark*, and I read Dickens. The opening line from his novel *A Tale of Two Cities*—"It was the best of times, it was the worst of times"—mirrors Richard's life. As Dickens employs foreshadowing in *A Tale of Two Cities*, the volatile summer of 1974 foreshadows Richard's career in Silicon Valley. He faces the worst economy since the Great Depression. It is the worst time to enter the technology industry, but it proves to be the best time for Richard.

After his first painstaking job search, subsequent job searches are a bit easier. His letters describe an exciting and scary time for the semiconductor industry, something out of the Wild West. He loves it.

Letter from Richard (1976):

Hi Mom,

After spending a year and a half at Drexler Technology / Microfab Systems Corporation, a semiconductor photomasking company in Palo

Alto, I have joined Fairchild Semiconductor—a huge company. I am now part of the Fairchild tribe.

Fairchild Semiconductor is rich in Silicon Valley folklore. It was founded in 1957 in Palo Alto by eight young engineers who left Shockley Semiconductor Laboratory in force, producing one of the Valley's first legendary stories. These eight young engineers turned their backs on their leader, William Shockley, who was awarded the Nobel Prize for his work developing the transistor. Shockley's harsh management style created an emotional environment, and these eight traitorous young engineers mutinied to form Fairchild Semiconductor, a division of Fairchild Camera and Instrument Corporation.

Mom, I love being a part of something important. This is history that should never be lost.

I am so proud of Richard. Although I don't always understand the content of his letters, they reflect an energy and excitement I have never seen in him.

After receiving this letter we have a follow-up call, and Richard says, "Mom, the Fairchildren—both the individuals and the companies spawned from Fairchild Semiconductor—have brought us some of the greatest technology companies in the world. The traitorous eight who launched Fairchild Semiconductor include such legends as Robert Noyce and Gordon Moore, the founders of Intel.

"Someone at work told me that a short paper written in July of 1945 by Dr. William Shockley suggested the economics of carnage favored deploying an atomic bomb versus invading Japan in World War II. How weird that he may have changed Dad's life, as well as mine."

Richard and I consistently talk via telephone over the next several years, allowing me to track his progress in Silicon Valley. In addition to our phone calls, he sends many letters. This one stands out:

Another letter from Richard (1976):

Hi Mom,

I want to see this stuff work—what semiconductors can do. Landing a financial analyst position within the Fairchild Semiconductor Video Game Group and working with Jerry Lawson is a dream come true.

Jerry Lawson is the group's director of engineering. What intrigues me most is Jerry Lawson the individual. He is friendly and very humble. He is the only Black engineer I've met while working at Fairchild Semiconductor. He is a member of the Homebrew Computer Club, a group of early computer hobbyists here in Silicon Valley.

Early club members also include Steve Jobs and Steve Wozniak, the founders of this year's fresh startup, Apple Computer. I sense a kinship with Jerry, as we are two of the few minorities I find working in the technology industry. When I come home for Christmas, I will share some amazing things that are rocking my world.

I love the rich details Richard provides in his letters. After I read them, the pain of our physical distance is somewhat relieved. Closing my eyes, I hear his letters as conversations. I miss our lengthy chats, which are limited due to the high cost of long-distance telephone service.

*   *   *

Richard arrives home on Christmas Eve with his car packed with several gifts. This year, his brightly wrapped parcels bring a glimpse into the future. I step outside to greet him. "Welcome home, Richard. Are you hungry from your long drive?"

"No, Mom, but I could use some help unloading my car."

I carry a few wrapped packages while Richard lugs his duffle bag of clothes. We walk through the back gate and up three steps, push open the back door, and then walk onto the back porch.

"Let's place the gifts under the tree for tomorrow morning," I say. I can't believe he actually wrapped presents this year.

Richard smiles and walks through the kitchen and into the living room. "Mom, I'm exhausted from the drive. Could we talk in the morning? Can I take my old bedroom?"

"It's ready."

Richard hauls his duffel bag down the hall, closes the bedroom door, and instantly turns out the light.

Early Christmas morning is reserved for the three of us. Other family members are coming over after lunch. When Set-chan and I get up and walk to the living room, Richard is sitting on the floor, having sorted out our gifts.

"Mom and Dad, Merry Christmas." He hands us a package wrapped in shiny green-and-red paper. "Please open this gift first. It's for you both."

Richard's magnetic spirit and energy warm the entire living room. I tear off the Scotch-taped paper to reveal a box with FAIRCHILD: VIDEO ENTERTAINMENT SYSTEM printed on it in big, bold letters. The picture on the box resembles a telephone answering machine I saw at one of my housecleaning jobs.

"Mom, let's hook it up to our television. It's in color," Richard blurts out.

I notice some plastic square boxes that resemble eight-track music cartridges. "What are these for?"

Richard laughs. "Those are the different game cartridges we can play on the entertainment system. We can play Casino Poker, Pro Football, and Racing Cars. This is so cool." He starts unpacking wires and funny-looking plastic tubes. Within minutes, our television is converted into a video racetrack with cars screaming down the speedway and crashing into each other.

Set-chan mumbles, "Can we play the Casino Poker game?"

"Sure." Richard fumbles to load the game cartridge. After it loads, Set-chan eagerly grabs the funny-looking plastic tubes to engage the dealer. Soon, four poker hands appear on screen and Set-chan's eyes light up. He places a bet and draws two cards, then calls. Two hands fold, and one hand raises the bet. Set-chan matches the raise, then calls. He wins with a full house. He's hooked.

Next, Richard presents two small, wrapped boxes to Set-chan and me. "These are special gifts for you both, to thank you for believing in me."

Set-chan opens his box first. It is a velvet jewelry box. He lifts one end to reveal a watch—instead of a dial, the face lights up with green numbers that indicate the time. When I unwrap and open my own velvet box, it contains a smaller watch with bright-red numbers lighting up the face.

"Oh, Richard! I can replace my old, beat-up Timex. The hands on the dial are so hard to see given my poor eyesight. These numbers are a bit odd to tell time with, but the red numbers are much easier to see. Thank you so much."

Richard nods and bursts out, "Dad, your watch has a liquid crystal display, and Mom, your watch has a light-emitting diode display. Our electronics power these watches. I wanted each of you to have one. Please wear them to remind you that I am thankful for your lessons, which enabled this dream to come true. I am helping to change the world."

Much slowly and softly, he says, "It's become clear to me that consumer electronics will be a high-volume user and future-growth catalyst for the semiconductor industry. This has whet my appetite for the virgin territory of personal computers."

"I love your enthusiasm, but what about the outdoors? Will technology help us improve our connection with nature? Dad and I continually reduce our time outdoors and absorb less natural sunlight and weather. We miss it. Remember the days we spent in the backyard shooting baskets or the days we spent going to the park? Those were some of our best memories."

"Mom, we can bring the outdoors indoor with technology."

"It's not the same, Richard."

"Maybe it could be better."

I think *maybe not*. Before I can fully absorb the holidays, it is time for Richard to drive back to San Jose.

* * *

In January 1977, Richard and I have a short telephone call that saddens me.

"Mom, I stopped dating. It's just too scary and expensive."

"Richard, is this your girlfriend from college? I really like her. She is a down-to-earth farm girl who lights up any room she occupies. I remember her smile when I asked about her parents and relatives. She led me back to my youth and how I truly miss living on a farm. Why did you break up?"

"I'm afraid. Sometimes I don't feel I am worthy of her, or anyone like her. The combination of being on my own, in debt from college, and hoping that nothing out of the ordinary goes wrong is stoking my fear of poverty. It's unbearable. It blocks any thought of being married or having children. Both elements—marriage and kids—have poverty written all over them."

I sigh and flash back to the frigid winter when we resettled in Utah after World War II. I understand his fear.

"I take my electronic handheld calculator to bed with me," Richard continues, "so if I awake in the middle of the night, which I do every night, I can punch in my budget for the month and read the harsh green numbers on the display. It provides a little comfort that I won't be living on the streets tomorrow. Next month is always in question."

"What about your friend Russ? Didn't he get married this year?" I ask.

"For Russ it's different. He has a functional and supportive family that can help him financially." He lets out a long, melancholy sigh. "Russ understands my situation and helps me forget about having a family and kids. Instead, he brings a smile to my face—he taught me how to ski like a 'hotdog' freestyler. Russ's parents live in Incline Village at Lake Tahoe, and I can stay there for free when we go skiing—although I must admit, playing blackjack in the casinos has paid for most of my skiing. And spending time with his family is great."

Richard perks up. "It is amazing, Mom. The fresh snow, the clean mountain air, and the exhilaration of conquering a mountainside full of bumps or moguls. I've learned advanced mogul techniques like avalement, swallowing the bumps while down unweighting, and quick wedeln turns. Without Russ's help, I'm sure I never would have learned to ski. He has opened so many doors I could not have entered without his help."

I smile—I am so happy that Richard has found such a great friend. Russ is truly his brother.

*   *   *

Letter from Richard (1979):

Hi Mom,

We are on the frontier of all humankind. We are modern day explorers of sorts. There are so many smart and well-educated people around me. I work hard to understand things, but sometimes I just can't. I am continually running, just to be left behind. I feel like I am unprepared for this battle. Still, even though I am a passenger, I love it.

A funny thing happened last week. I was walking down a hallway when two friends approached me. They were grumbling about competition from Japanese companies.

"Richard," one of them said, "can you tell your people to slow down their new products? They are killing our business."

"My people?" I said.

"Yeah, your people. Aren't you Japanese?"

I laughed and walked away. I don't think they were serious.

Anyway, Fairchild Semiconductor has been sold to Schlumberger, and it's not the same. I've accepted the corporate controller's job at Commodore Business Machines, Inc. (CBM). Their PC, the PET (Personal Electronic Transactor), is a direct competitor to Apple Computer's Apple II and Tandy / Radio Shack's TRS-80—the three PCs that make up the 1977 trinity.

I was told by the president that I need to be a tough guy and not take any shit from the staff. I shared your story about being tough and birthing two daughters in the WWII camps here in America, and about the power and spirit of Bushido. The president went silent. He then mumbled something about "Auschwitz" and said, "I understand," and walked away.

Richard is applying what we discussed in the summer of 1973; he is building accomplishments beyond reproach. I am afraid. I don't want my child with the amazing heart to lose it. Technology may be advancement, but it could also be an irreversible, unsympathetic destructive force. I hope his

Bushido lessons ground him and his outdoor interests like skiing keep him connected to the real world of nature.

159

15

Four Tears of Life

Throughout my life, my tears have been the common denominator. My tears capture my escalating emotions of fear, sorrow, joy, and hope. My tears open my heart and enable me to pass on my *ikigai*. My tears project an understanding of the pivotal moments of my life. As sequencing these events chronologically quells the confusion within my brain, this chapter shares the natural evolution of my tears—from the fear of not knowing, to the sorrow of loss, to the joy of happiness and pride, to the spiritual, healing power of hope.

Tears of Fear

In 1981, my son Richard tells me the computer world has flipped a switch. In August of that year, International Business Machines (IBM) introduces its PC, legitimizing the personal computer.

"I'm not scared yet," he says, "but I am in a section of the technology industry where the lights are beginning to dim."

Over the next several years, I see Richard trying to find his way. After working at Fairchild Semiconductor and CBM, he experiments with several startup companies. They all fail. The last of these startups sells for pennies on the dollar.

Overnight, in 1986, Richard loses everything: his job, his investments in these companies, and his home. He becomes a transient, not knowing where he will find shelter. His options are to live in his car or in cheap motels, or to couch surf at friends' places. I am fearful, not knowing if he will survive. At thirty-three years old, he is no child, and Set-chan, to my dismay, tests his *gaman*—a word in Japanese culture that describes enduring unbearable conditions with dignity and patience.

Letter from Richard (February 1986):

Hi Mom,

My first vice president position has been a twenty-four-month sharp downward spiral. The recent fire sale of my technology startup company resulted in the loss of my job, with no severance pay. I am nearly broke. My investments have vanished, I am in credit card hell, the girl I was dating dumped me, and I lost my condo. I have minimal cash reserves, as I thought this would be the startup that succeeded. Wrong again. I have abandoned looking for health insurance. I have learned that debt and risk are both four-letter words.

This morning, I was awakened by the constant swoosh of cars rushing past the only door to my cheap motel room. My alarm clock failed its purpose by stopping in the middle of the night—face-

less and dark, unlike the morning outside. Waking puffy-eyed and unrested, I heard the small room refrigerator whirl for a moment, then go silent. Dressed in my sweatpants, I reached over to flip the switch for the overhead light. A short, brilliant flash signaled the death of another light bulb. I opened the curtains to the view of an asphalt parking lot and the backside of a fast-food restaurant. Beyond the tattered tar is El Camino Real Boulevard, one of the busiest streets in Santa Clara.

When I returned to Northern California after the holidays, I was couch surfing in the East Bay. But not wanting to overstay my welcome, I moved back to Silicon Valley in late January. This meant moving my possessions into storage and selling my stereo system to generate cash. I kept three suits for interviewing and two pictures, which help me fight loneliness. At the February flea market in South San Jose, I sold my television, my old computer, my printer, half of my clothes, and whatever small furniture people could physically take away.

Mom, I may miss your birthday next month on March 20—I'm sorry.

Letter from Richard (March 1986):
Hi Mom,

Happy belated birthday. Sorry I missed it. I am living part-time in a cheap Santa Clara motel and using my car as a second room. I pay $172.50 every other week for the motel room. It is somewhat clean, but the carpet is crunchy and I dare not walk on it barefoot. I have a hot plate for cooking, a small refrigerator, and a small television to keep me company.

I am still unemployed and looking for anything. I have been turned down for part-time work by retail stores and gas stations—they claimed I was over-qualified. With no income, I am stretching my cash and selling anything of value at the flea markets.

My storage unit is getting bigger and bigger as my list of possessions gets smaller and smaller. I have sold pretty much everything that anyone will buy. At the end of this month, I will terminate my storage-unit lease to save money and move the remaining stuff into my car. I've kept my Jack LaLanne gym membership so I'll have a place to shower and brush my teeth when I'm not staying in a motel. As I don't have a phone or physical address in Northern California, I posted your phone number and address on my resume. If it's okay, I will call you every Monday evening, collect, to see if anyone has responded to my job-search letters.

I still struggle with my inner poverty voice. When I wake up in the middle of the night, I am faced by the menacing glow of my calculator display, its green light taunting me. I lie there in the dark, picturing that perfect origami flower you made for me in 1967, and try to imagine my life as I would like to see it. Thanks, Mom.

Letter from Richard (May 1986):

Hi Mom,

The warmer weather has opened up cheaper living options. I have been sleeping in my yellow Volkswagen Bug when I can find secluded parking spots. On many nights, as I stretch out in the back seat, my overactive imagination keeps me awake. I envision strangers shattering my car windows to steal what I have left of my life.

I was trained to save face, to respect myself. I was trained to be mentally strong. I was not trained to be alone. I try to find the right voices—the sensitive, thoughtful, and soft voices. I reach inside myself, trying not to hit bottom. But I have.

I am self-destructing. I have lost my self-respect, my confidence, my desire to go on. Although at no time have I considered doing anything illegal, the inner voice of poverty has become a constant companion, occasionally drowned out by the louder, angry voices of fear. Fear now haunts me, in the dark and the light. Increasingly, I sit motionless on the corner of my motel bed or in my VW and look deep inside myself, only to find an empty shell. Mom, I'm drowning up here.

When I receive this letter, fear strikes me. I approach Set-chan as he sits in his dilapidated chair in the living room, reading the Japanese newspaper *Rafu Shimpo*.

"Set-chan, please read this letter." My voice does not waver. "It scares me."

Set-chan quietly reads. When he finishes, he places the letter on the TV tray by his chair and slowly looks up. "Richard is not coming home to live with us. Although he is welcome to visit."

"Set-chan, this is our son—"

"Richard is a man. If he is to be a real man, he must weather this time and learn from it. He is not coming home."

I don't want to lose my mystical son. But as I walk away, I follow Set-chan's lead. I shove my fear behind my anger and hold steady.

Then comes the June letter.

> **Letter from Richard (June 1986):**
>
> *Mom,*
>
> *My growing depression has led to suicidal thoughts. Another birthday—I am now thirty-four, with nothing meaningful in my life. I have truly found bottom. I clutch the origami flower you made for me in 1967. I clutch my Smith & Wesson .357 Magnum revolver.*
>
> *Staring at the yellowing origami flower, I sit and spin the loaded cylinder in my revolver and click it into place. I hold both the flower and my gun close to my heart. No one but me would want the old origami flower. The flower is my hope—the light in my life. My revolver is my escape—the darkness in my life. They are now my two best friends.*
>
> *I continue exploring all across California, looking for work. It has been six months. This week food will take priority over staying in a motel. After this month I will have nothing left to sell. I always said*

that if I were to leave Silicon Valley, I would take what I could pack in my car, just as I did when I came here. I now realize that this may come true.

My poverty voice has gained volume, while my voice of sanity gasps for help. I am tired. Mom, will Dad consider letting me come home?

I get up from my makeshift desk in our bedroom and walk down the hallway, thinking about what I want to say to Set-chan, sitting in his chair.

I approach him head-on and say again, "Set-chan, please read this letter from Richard."

He quietly extends his hand, and I place it firmly onto his palm. As he reads, he begins mumbling. After a few minutes, he puts down the letter.

"Richard is a man and must act like one."

I hold back my anger but not my tears. "Set-chan, enough. What good will it do for him to reach a point of no return?"

Set-chan does not respond. I stand in front of him, hands on my hips and foot tapping the threadbare carpet.

The silence is finally broken by his short reply. "I will talk to him next Monday evening."

Nothing more is said.

That Monday evening, the heavy black phone in the kitchen rings. I pick it up and am greeted by a telephone operator.

"Will you accept a collect call from Richard Okumoto?"

"Yes," I quickly respond.

A moment of silence, and then Richard quietly mumbles, "Hi, Mom . . . How are you?"

"I am fine, but Dad would like to talk with you, okay?" I rush out.

A heavy sigh from Richard. "Yep, sure."

Hearing the telephone conversation, Set-chan gets up from his living room chair and limps into the kitchen. I look at him, filled with hope that he will ease my pain and welcome my son home.

Set-chan fumbles and picks up the handset. "Richard, I am told you are whining."

My anger flares and I want to hit Set-chan.

"You have graduated college, you are able-bodied, you speak English, you are in your home country," he continues. "Why are you complaining? Why are you so weak? Are you telling me that my nearly six-foot, two-hundred-pound son is weaker than his five-foot-two-inch, one-hundred-twenty-five-pound father? Are you telling me you are not strong? I did not go to college, I speak broken English, and I struggled through five operations over nine years to learn how to walk again. Are you telling me your struggles are greater? No, you will not tell me that. You have no *gaman*."

At this, I begin to cry.

Set-chan continues pushing, shouting, "Tell me—"

Before he can finish his sentence, Richard interrupts. "I have *gaman*." He repeats, "I have *gaman*."

A muffled thud reverberates from the other end of the phone. Horrified, I realize Richard has hung up the telephone. The line goes dead. My body shivers in shock at what has just happened.

Set-chan slowly places the handset onto its cradle. He looks down. "I must know if he can do it. I must know if he is a man. If Richard fails, then we have failed. I need to know he can survive on his own. He will survive." He says no more and hobbles out of the kitchen.

Stunned, I cry harder. *What if he can't do it? Am I to stand by and watch my mystical son perish?* But I know my place and quietly shuffle off to my bedroom.

Days turn into weeks with no contact from Richard. My anger grows and my sadness absorbs all my energy. I have lost faith in Set-chan. He stoically never speaks another word about the telephone call.

The third Sunday morning after our last call with Richard, the telephone rings in the kitchen. I run to answer it, petrified that it will be a horrible call from a hospital or the police.

I pick up the handset and am greeted with "Will you accept a collect call from Richard Okumoto?"

"Yes, yes, I will."

I cannot wait for him to speak. "Richard, are you okay? We were worried when we did not hear from you for so long."

Richard talks slowly, in a monotone voice. "Mom, I am okay. I would like to read my letter to you and Dad. I didn't want you to wait until I mailed it."

I drop the telephone handset and run into the living room to get Set-chan. "Set-chan, Set-chan, it's Richard, come quickly."

He slowly stands up from his chair and shuffles into the kitchen. Sharing the telephone handset, we listen to Richard as he reads out loud.

Letter from Richard (July 1986):

During one of my lost evenings, I saw Dad walking. I saw him forfeit nine years of his life to walk again. He showed me what resilience looks like. At five foot two, how did he become so strong? How did he and Mom survive the years in the war camps? How did they find belief beyond the barbed-wire fences?

In Silicon Valley it doesn't matter what you have done, unless it was yesterday or today when you achieved success. Fear runs everyone's life. The intense competition has laid the foundation for mass paranoia. Everyone knows what everyone else is doing, going to do, or would like to do. Becoming a has-been is just a short breath from your last. If you aren't involved in working on the next big thing, you are passé. It is an adrenaline junkie's paradise. All that said, I hate it but cannot get enough of it.

The night after my call with you and Dad, I stretched out on a towel covering the hood of my yellow VW Bug. I closed my eyes, hoping to shut out the world and find calm. When I woke the next morning and found myself curled up on the back seat of the car, I realized a summer dream had caught me by surprise. Instead of running in fear, I felt a quiet peace. At that moment, I was the only judge of who I am. I calmly faced my loaded .357 Magnum, cradling it in both arms. I looked into the barrel and saw daylight skimming along the spiraling grooves within. It was this glistening spiral that led me to my inner self. It was here that I found the truth in my life.

Cautiously, I swung open the loaded revolver cylinder. I used the pushrod to carefully unload my revolver. After six cartridges had fallen to the ground, I pushed the cylinder back into place and heard it click. Without questioning, I pointed the gun to my head and closed my eyes. I instinctively pulled the double-action trigger. After hearing the snap of the hammer hitting the empty chamber, I opened my eyes to see the world and proclaimed, "I am still here, and the darkness is gone."

That morning, I walked with honor and strength and reestablished my routine. The following mornings I found myself up at 7 a.m. and off to the gym. By 10 a.m. I was researching companies with possible job openings in accounting or operations.

There was no self-help book or guru pulling me into nirvana. There were no mind-altering drugs. I simply recalibrated my needs in life. It is no longer a new car or a large home that makes me happy, but breathing air—yes, air. Now, every day, I smile deep inside and feel calm and joy. I smile at each sunrise and laugh—yes, I laugh—at each sunset. My origami flower smiles at me and reminds me not to fear uncertainty. I feel sorry for those who shun me. I look directly into everyone's eyes as if they are mine.

I found joy just sitting on my yellow VW, watching the wind catching leaves and tossing them into the air. As I sat there, I just smiled. Another smile followed, and then another. I began tapping my feet to the rhythm of songs on my AM car radio. I laughed at my mismatched socks and my broken shoelaces.

Shortly thereafter, something else happened. After hundreds of resumes and countless first interviews, I landed a second interview. A British company is looking for someone to manage its software business in the United States. Subsequent interviews went well. I received a job offer requiring I start work in two weeks.

I will be entering the television newsroom software automation industry. The company is called Basys, Inc., and it is a division of ITN (Independent Television News) out of London. After living on the streets for nearly seven months, I will now be managing a small business division. We will rock the newsroom industry, from RTNDA (Radio Television News Director Association) to NAB (National Association of Broadcasters) trade shows. We will automate newsroom operations, from story development to incorporating electronic wire feeds directly into computers, eliminating the clicking teletypes, and feeding them into the teleprompter. We will organize news material that is read by the on-air news talent. Seeing the technology applied will be awesome.

My next stops will be television newsrooms around the nation, filled with news anchors and producers. My new places of work will include New York, Atlanta, London, Washington, DC, Boston, and San Francisco. I will spend two to three weeks on the road each month. I am told the Omni Atlanta Hotel will become my second home during our upgrade installation at CNN.

I have rented a one-bedroom apartment in San Jose on a month-to-month basis with the hopes this job will stick. I desperately need a place I can call home.

Richard says, "I wrote these words in my green notebook: 'Those select few who retain their dreams through the many ordeals of life will be the creative geniuses of tomorrow.' Thank you, Mom and Dad, for believing in me. I do have *gaman*."

My tears, stemming from the fear of not knowing, now cement my understanding of Richard's journey to become a man. Set-chan's approach to overcoming this fear has worked. As I place the telephone handset onto its cradle, Set-chan smiles and shuffles back to the living room in silence.

Tears of Sorrow

Sundays are usually calm and quiet. Set-chan has been complaining about not feeling well. Maybe it is the heat and humidity of this summer morning that is aggravating his system. He scuttles off to the back of the house while I sit in the living room, sewing a rip in his only white dress shirt. I want to make sure he has a presentable dress shirt for today, June 21, 1992, Father's Day. After tying off the last stitch, I fluff the shirt and realize I need to iron it. I get up from my chair, walk to the back porch, and pull out the ironing board from the tall closet. As I plug in the iron, my nose fills with the harsh tobacco scent emanating from underneath the door of the bathroom off the back porch. It is closed, so I knock twice, knowing what to expect.

A low cough sounds, and then a gruff voice says, "I'm busy. Use the other bathroom."

I knock again. Silence follows.

The bathroom door opens and Set-chan stands in his work pants, reeking of cigarette smoke. Startled, he looks down, knowing he is in big trouble.

"Set-chan, were you smoking in the bathroom?" I do not raise my voice, only alter its pitch and projection.

His face turns into a bright-red, rising sun. This glow is well beyond embarrassment and signals his blood pressure is very high. "Only one," he mutters, his face becoming paler as he calms down.

What a pain! I think. *He's just like a rebellious little child.*

I begin laughing. "Set-chan, it's Sunday, Father's Day. I want to treat you to dinner at Mesa Restaurant."

"I don't feel like going," he mumbles as he walks to his heavily worn recliner chair in the living room. He turns ashen. I worry he may be catching a cold or the flu. "Just tired," he says, before falling asleep in his chair.

Sunday passes quickly, and I redirect my energies to prepare for work on Monday.

Awakened by heat and high humidity the next day, I eagerly depart early to clean Mrs. D's air-conditioned home in San Marino. It's an escape from the dreaded heat of our home, where the bars on the windows prevent us from opening them. These bars both protect us and imprison us. I suppose this is a fair tradeoff.

I am looking forward to chatting with Set-chan about the possibility of getting a secondhand air-conditioning unit for one room in the house. Mrs. D suggested the Salvation Army store might have a cheap room air-conditioning unit. Upon arriving home I park in the driveway, intending to manually open the garage door and then park in the garage. Stepping out of my car, I hear an engine running. When I open the garage door, Set-chan's truck is parked in the center of the garage with the engine idling—so odd. Annoyed, I walk from the garage to the back door of our house—it is unlocked. How strange! I open the door and nearly stumble over Set-chan, who is lying on the floor, contorted and dribbling.

"Set-chan! Set-chan!" I cry out his name, trying to get his attention.

His eyes roll back and close as he mumbles something and then passes out. Based on his body position, it looks like he fell and couldn't get up. I rush to the telephone and call for an ambulance. It is 5:30 p.m.

The paramedics arrive within fifteen minutes and quickly examine Set-chan. "Mrs. Okumoto, we're transporting your husband to Huntington Memorial for further examination."

"What is wrong with him? What happened?"

"We're not sure, but we will know more after the hospital doctors have a chance to see him." The paramedic is kind and direct.

I grab a few things and then scurry off to the hospital.

Arriving at the hospital, I feel a chill. I hate hospitals. The attending nurse informs me they are running tests to determine what happened to Set-chan, and I wait patiently. I am the only person sitting in the sterile, white waiting room. As my anxiety settles, I am assailed by a flurry of questions. *What if Set-chan dies? What if he had a heart attack? What if he is mentally disabled?* So many thoughts run through my head. At 9:30 p.m., two doctors emerge through the double doors.

"Mrs. Okumoto," the older doctor addresses me.

"Yes."

"Your husband appears to have suffered a major stroke."

Bewildered, I break down crying, and the doctor stops talking and waits for a moment before continuing.

"Mrs. Okumoto, we will need to keep your husband overnight for observation, and we will conduct more tests tomorrow morning. We should have the results of his blood tests at that time."

"May I see him?"

"He's resting comfortably now. It appears he has lost control of his right side, which is showing signs of paralysis. His neck is very tight—that may have been caused by a TIA, a prestroke seizure—and we are checking for blood clots. We'll know more tomorrow. I suggest you go home and get some rest. Tomorrow will be a long day for you."

"Thank you, Doctor."

In a daze, I walk out of the hospital and to my parked car. Fumbling with my car keys, I lean on the car and begin to cry. How did this happen? I sit in the car, not moving, for several minutes. But I must get home. As I drive, wondering what the future will look like, I feel panicked. It is dark when I arrive home; I forgot to turn on the lights. Walking from room to room, I leave a trail of bright lights, illuminating my emptiness. I remember the doctor's comment and ask myself, "How can I fall asleep now?"

Not able to sleep, I make a list of everyone I need to call. I write down my thoughts on what I need to do next. When I look up from my makeshift desk in the bedroom, the sun is beginning its journey across the backyard, exposing dark corners of the garden and the cinder-block wall that marks the end of our yard. As I walk toward the kitchen with my call list, solitude overtakes me. I stop short and sit in the living room to collect my thoughts.

Is this really happening? I ask myself.

I make one call after another, focusing on the mechanical action of contacting relatives who live in close proximity. Richard calls, breaking through my numbness. This is his normal every-other-day call—now that Set-chan and I live alone, he calls on a regular basis. We chat about next steps.

"Mom, I will immediately ask for time off work so I can come down to help sort things out."

"Thank you, Richard." I drop the phone.

The afternoon is lost in a repetitive refrain: "We are so sorry, Mary, and please let us know what we can do to help."

Tuesday becomes Wednesday, and I cancel work on both days. I return to the hospital, where doctors sit me down so I can absorb the update.

"We are now certain your husband had a major stroke. We have a physical therapist and speech pathologist working with him today. It is important to understand, whatever capabilities he regains this week will more than likely be what he will have going forward."

From my journal (Wednesday, June 24, 1992):

Busy, hot day. At Huntington Hospital before 8 a.m. to see Dr. Kunetake. She has scheduled physical therapy for Set-chan. He was angry and scoffed during our entire conversation. We were interrupted by Karen at Huntington Medical Group. She came to inform me that she has made it possible for him to go to Alderwood Manor Convalescent Hospital in San Gabriel tomorrow for rehabilitation. I spent the entire day working to get him admitted. That evening, Richard called and said he is coming down this Sunday through next Tuesday to help me.

From my journal (Thursday, June 25, 1992): *It was a warm, not-too-hot day. I needed to go to work and earn some money to pay for things Set-chan needs during his stay at the convalescent hospital. After work I went to Sears Department Store and bought pajamas, slippers, and underwear (without holes, like his older ones) for him. When I arrived at the convalescent hospital, Set-chan had on borrowed clothes that were just too big. He looked so funny sitting in his wheelchair. When he saw me, he began grinning and laughing. He seemed more hopeful. I am so grateful for the orderlies who made him laugh.*

The next few days are filled with telephone calls and visits from my sisters, Set-chan's sister, and our nephew Kenny. I talk with Richard two to three times a day, laying out what my next steps should be. Each night after leaving Set-chan, I sit at home, envisioning his withered body and crying as I replay how he struggles so hard to do anything: speaking, eating, or just wiggling his toes. Set-chan is now a prisoner in his own body. I can see his mind working, but his body does not respond. What torture for him to endure.

Three days pass. Today I bring Set-chan home. It is overcast, as if the sky is sad. Set-chan is quiet and somber.

Richard and I agree that I need in-home help to care for Set-chan. We interview and hire Oshiro-san to come in five days a week to help me. We also agree that I need to stop working. I panic at this thought, but Richard assures me that our finances will be okay, and when our funds run short, he will cover us. Thirty years later, I am again caring for Set-chan. Only this time he has lost many of his capabilities, and I have lost my partner.

For the remainder of 1992, Richard either flies or drives from Silicon Valley to Pasadena each weekend. When Christmas comes, Richard brings a friend, Kim, whom he met at work. Their visit warms our holiday. Kim is a sweet, shy, petite blonde. I like her demeanor and grounded nature. She and I talk about her Navy family—her dad is a retired Navy commander and fighter pilot who was the third flight leader for the Navy Blue Angels. I am not certain about their relationship, but I like her.

I mention to Richard that I have sold everything that is not being used or is not a family heirloom: Set-chan's truck and work tools, the piano, the sewing machine. One item remains—an item I cherish but have difficulties playing, as my fingers are tired and they often hurt when I apply pressure to them. This is my Japanese *koto*, a long, wooden musical instrument.

Richard says numerous times, "Mom, if it gives you joy, even if you can no longer play it, keep it. If it makes you smile to see it, keep it. I am interviewing for a new job that starts in February 1993, and it will pay a lot more money. I can cover your cash shortfalls. Don't worry."

* * *

After the start of the new year, I stare at my *koto*, smile, and say, "Enough." In February 1993, I sell it to a lady called June Kuramoto. During a phone call with Richard in the second week of March, I mention the sale of my *koto*. A deafening silence follows, and I envision him sitting there, a bit stunned.

With the wonderment of a child, Richard asks, "Mom, do you know who June Kuramoto is?"

I shrug my shoulders. "No."

"When I come down this weekend, I'll bring a few compact discs, CDs, so you can hear her play," Richard blurts out.

Okay, June has recorded a CD. How nice, I think.

On my birthday, Saturday, March 20, 1993, I sit motionless in the living room, listening to the CDs Richard brought with him during his ritual weekend trip to visit me. The amazing sound of a fast-moving, electrified *koto* fills the room with music from the band Hiroshima.

Shocked and proud, I whisper, "This is a great home for my *koto*, and I am proud of its future."

"Mom, please keep these Hiroshima CDs so you can hear what your *koto* can produce under the hands of June Kuramoto," Richard says.

I quickly accept. "Richard, this is a gift that I will always cherish. Thank you."

* * *

March turns into April, and Richard is working long hours at his new company, Credence Systems Corporation, where he is the new chief financial officer (CFO). Due to his workload, he can only come down to Pasadena every other weekend. But no matter how tired he is, he always comes every other weekend to help me.

As May approaches, Richard prepares me for the likelihood that he may only be able to come down once a month for a while. Starting in June, his workload may require him to work for months without any time off, except possibly Sundays. He mentions that he is doing something all CFOs want to do: an initial public offering, or IPO.

When he visits on May 22, clearly fatigued, he struggles to get out these words: "Mom, I am going to be unavailable to visit for a few months. We are four months from taking our company public, and I will be literally living at my office and at the printer's office."

He looks so tired. I am worried about him and suggest he rests. He trudges off to his old bedroom to lie down. That afternoon turns into evening as Richard sleeps for fifteen hours.

On June 10, I am hesitant to call Richard, but it is his birthday. Luckily, he calls me.

"Mom, I will be attending an executive off-site meeting in the Santa Cruz Mountains from tomorrow, Friday, until this Sunday morning, June 13. I'll call you when I get back and let you know how things are going."

Richard drifts on for a bit, but I want Richard to get some sleep, so I cut our call short.

On Sunday morning, June 13, I work in the garden. Taking a break, I step into the house and sit down at the kitchen table. I look over at the telephone answering machine sitting on the kitchen counter. In bright-red, glowing letters, it says "NO MESSAGES." Oshiro-san is in the bedroom, tending to Set-chan, and I walk down the hall to check on them.

"Oshiro-san, were there any telephone calls while I was outside?"

She stops feeding Set-chan and looks up. "Mary, I did not hear the telephone ring."

"Hmm."

I grunt and walk back to the kitchen, sit at the table, and eat one slice of toast. After my short break, I go back outside to tend my garden. The cloudy sky hides the sun's movement, and two o'clock sneaks up on me. Thirsty, I decide I've had enough and it is time to rest.

Expecting a telephone message, I check the answering machine. Again, no messages. Now, I am panicked. I call Richard, and when he answers I can barely get the words out. "Richard, are you okay? I expected to hear from you this morning. Is everything all right?"

I hear muffled crying and sniffling. Richard clears his throat and says he is okay. Then, he breaks down. "Mom, Russ Fisher and his dad crashed their airplane this morning—"

"Are they hurt? Are they badly hurt?"

Richard is silent. Then he takes a deep breath. "Mom, they crashed into South Lake Tahoe. They are both dead. I just can't believe they are dead. Russ and his dad are dead."

Russ has been Richard's best friend and his real brother for twenty years.

Richard rambles on, "I flash on Russ's wedding plans with Chrissy—it was planned for this fall, only four months away. I see us skiing moguls at Squaw Valley. I see his face as we hike the hills in Incline Village during the summer months. I feel him lifting me up as I struggle from a fall on my mountain bike. Russ can't be dead. He just turned forty two weeks ago." He begins to sob.

I quickly respond, "Richard, is it better to continue talking, or do you need to be by yourself?"

"Mom, I should go and regroup. Thank you for listening." But he keeps on talking. "I need to fly to Reno tomorrow to identify the bodies, along with his mom, his sister, and his brother. June 13 will always be a day of sadness for me. When Russ was in Australia, an Aboriginal fortune teller told him that he saw a Japanese warrior walking in Russ's past life. Maybe that's why we were best friends. I just can't believe they are gone. Mom, I'm sorry, I've got to go."

The phone goes dead, and there is an eerie silence, after which a dial tone pops up, signaling our call has ended.

Several days pass, and I record a mystifying incident in my journal.

> From my journal (Wednesday, June 16, 1993):
>
> *For some reason I can't sleep. Odd, it feels so cold this morning. After tossing in bed for a while, at 3 a.m. I get up to work in the garden adjacent to our outdoor pond. An hour after the sun rises, at about 8 a.m., with Oshiro-san's help, I decide to get Set-chan up and ready for breakfast. I enter Set-chan's bedroom and find him crying. His eyes teary, through tortured lips he mumbles, "Richard came home to attend his friend's funeral and was all broken up."*

Strange. How would Set-chan know this?

Later that afternoon, Richard calls me. I tell him about Dad's early-morning comments. A few moments of silence follow. Then, Richard tells me about his past few days and reluctantly relates his early-morning experience today.

"Mom, I went to Reno on Monday to visit Russ's mom and sister. On Tuesday we all went to the funeral parlor to identify the bodies of Russ and his dad. The attendants brought in two dark-green body bags—they appeared greasy or slick—placed them on two separate tables, and slowly unzipped the body bags. Russ's dad was unrecognizable. But Russ looked peaceful." After a short pause, Richard continues, "Mom, I stared at him, hoping he would wake up and tell me this was an elaborate hoax. Seconds turned into minutes, and my legs began to feel weak. I had to quickly leave the room and go outside, where I immediately threw up my breakfast. The remainder of the day was a blur."

Richard takes a deep breath and goes on. "I was staying in the downstairs bedroom in Russ's house that night. Around 2:30 a.m. I was lying in the dark, unable to sleep. Then I began to shiver, not from cold, but from fear. I can't explain what I was afraid of, but I knew I was afraid of something. This continued for a while as I lay motionless in bed. Finally, I said out loud, 'Russ, knock

Russ, his dad, and Richard at the Narita Airport two years before the fatal plane crash

it off.... You're scaring me.' At 3:00 a.m. I turned on the bedroom light and the fear faded. Still unable to sleep, I got up, packed, and drove to the Reno airport to catch my flight home to the Bay Area.... Mom, maybe Russ—his energy force—was traveling from Reno to Pasadena to let us know he is okay now and will always be here."

Richard closes our call by saying, "Russ is no longer by my side to help me focus. Mom, I am not sure if I can pick up the pieces. It's just too much—taking my company public is placing enormous demands on me, and now I've lost my best friend." A dial tone follows.

Alone, sitting in the kitchen, I shed tears of sorrow over our losses: the loss of the soul of my life partner, Set-chan, and Richard's loss of his best friend and true brother.

Tears of Joy

Days go by and I don't hear from Richard. June becomes July before we talk again. Each call thereafter is no more than two or three minutes. The topic is always what I need to care for Set-chan. Richard never mentions work or Russ. In early August, that changes.

"We scattered Russ's fluorescent ashes in the lake yesterday morning," Richard says. "His words echoed in my head— move on and live your life. That afternoon, I sat for hours by myself in my hotel room in Incline Village and stared out at Lake Tahoe. I closed my eyes and told myself that Russ came into my life so I could understand and appreciate true friendship. It is time to continue. But ... I miss him."

"Death creates a physical emptiness," I say. "But in your heart you will never lose him. Feel the sadness and remember the joy. Both make you human. Both give you balance. Yes, it is time."

In September, during a short telephone call, Richard says, "Mom, I may be unreachable in October. This is it. We must complete the IPO by the end of October. This will be a brutal time for me."

Richard is true to his word. We talk on the telephone only once in October. The letter he sends in November captures his prior month's journey.

Letter from Richard (Sunday, November 7, 1993):

Hi Mom,

I wrote this down because I know if we have a telephone call, I will be rambling the entire time. I am just so tired. I can't believe I survived these past eight months. Writing this letter gives me time to reflect on my recent journey. Sometimes—well, many times—I can't believe it happened.

Woody Spedden, the CEO of Credence Systems, and I started our relationship with a handshake at the Lion & Compass restaurant in the heart of Silicon Valley. This iconic location is where I accepted the position of chief financial officer, working with Woody to take Credence Systems public. It's only now that I fully appreciate the journey we were about to embark upon.

Together, we honed our presentation and discussion skills, training under Jerry Weissman—an amazing person. It was a grueling few weeks. I learned so much from Jerry. While that was happening, the management team focused on sharpening our internal controls and preparing the mountain of documents and information we needed to disclose. My specific focus was reorganizing the European operations, generating positive cash flow, nailing down our financial model, and working with the investment bankers, corporate attorneys, and public accountants. It was long days and long nights that found me sleeping in my office and at the office of the printer that prepared our legal documents.

All that work culminated in Woody and me going on the road to talk to prospective investors—a whirl-wind tour in the United States and Europe, which came to a fitting end in London. We needed to get back to New York before the next morning to price the deal. To accomplish this, our investment bankers presented Woody and me with British Airways (BA) tickets on the Concorde.

Woody and I flew transatlantic, from London's Heathrow Airport to New York's JFK Airport, as passengers on the BA Concorde jet. We crossed the Atlantic Ocean in just over three hours, at an altitude of sixty thousand feet and at twice the speed of sound. Mom, we were flying faster than the earth's rotational speed.

What an amazing conclusion to our work. I am thankful to both Woody and you for believing in me.

After reading this letter, I shed tears of joy. Richard's rise to Silicon Valley executive is a miracle. Just seven years ago, he was living in his car and in cheap motels. I am so happy and proud of him. I designed an ikebana arrangement in which the middle and lower parts, the *soe* and the *hikae*, reflect Richard's grounding in humility. Viewing this brings a part of him into my home, every day.

Tears of Hope

In late January 1994, while sitting at the kitchen table, I have a telephone conversation with Richard.

"Mom, while presenting at an investor conference in New York City earlier this month, I noticed a lump on my throat. It was bitter cold, with snow still on the ground. The chilly weather aggravated my throat and numbed any sensation from the lump, but upon my return to Northern California, I could clearly see an oblong growth on the right-front side of my neck."

Is this a harbinger of his health? Shaken, I ask, "What does this mean? Have you seen a doctor yet?"

"The swelling may be caused by a virus or something else. I have a sore throat. I went to the doctor and was prescribed antibiotics. That will help. Nothing to worry about."

I am relieved. I worry about his health as Richard talks about the long hours he is working, his extensive travel schedule, and the constant stress he is under. I hear fatigue in his voice.

February, March, and April slip by,

Tome and one of her sisters, Richard's Ikebana

and Richard mentions the lump is continuing to grow. During a May telephone call, he discusses a change to his treatment.

"The needle biopsy, the ultrasound, and the iodine uptake procedures indicate I may have abnormal cell activity in my thyroid. I scheduled a partial thyroidectomy for August 22."

As I sit in the kitchen, listening to him describe his course of action, my heart sinks. I struggle to understand what I just heard.

"Richard, is it cancer?"

He hesitates. "It may be thyroid cancer. The doctors have to operate before they can form a final prognosis."

Panic sets in. *Why does my son have cancer at forty-two years old?* I ask why he doesn't schedule the operation sooner.

Richard swallows, and then there is a brief silence. "Mom, my workload is horrendous. Our second-quarter financial results must be ready by the end of June, and I need to prepare the press release. After the public disclosure, there is a conference call with investors in the second week of August. Monday, August 22, is the earliest I can have the operation."

I sigh. "You know best, but I worry."

The days following that terrible telephone conversation are hot and humid. June becomes July, and in the last days of July, sitting on my worn chair in the kitchen, I receive a call from Richard. He is working on Saturday and Sunday, as usual.

"Mom, I'll be ready for my operation next month. The growth on my neck seems to be slowing down . . . maybe just wishful thinking."

Maintaining a positive attitude, I declare, "It will be good, I know it."

After hanging up the phone I sit motionless—there is nothing else I can do. I walk outside to bask in the heat of the Pasadena summer day. I close my eyes and see the boys taking jump shots at the makeshift basketball hoop we assembled in the backyard. They are so young. Their smiles are so clear in my memory. Losing any one of my children would kill me. Losing my mystical son would be devastating. This can't and won't happen—not after all the bad that has already happened in my life. This can't happen.

> **From my journal (Monday, August 22, 1994):**
>
> *Lovely weather today. Oshiro-san arrived early to help me with Set-chan. Getting him up, to the bathroom, and to the kitchen table for breakfast is our standard morning ritual. After breakfast I sit outside, taking deep breaths before the smog replaces the fresh morning air. I wait for a call updating me about Richard.*

When the telephone rings, I run into the house, nearly tripping along the way.

Kim's low, resonant voice greets me. "Hi, Mary, Richard is doing fine." She sounds exhausted. "The operation went well. They tested a frozen sample of the removed portion of his thyroid, and it looks okay. Not exactly sure what that means. We will know more tomorrow. I apologize, but I must cut this short—I have a long list of calls to make."

I am relieved to know Kim is there to take care of him. They have had their ups and downs, but in the end, she is there for him. Like Richard, Kim works long hours in the technology industry. They are two kids trying to sort out their lives and the crazy demands of their work schedules.

"Kim, thank you for taking care of Richard. I deeply appreciate your help."

Kim starts to cry. "Mary, it is so horrible seeing Richard this way. He is suffering, but he will never tell you. He will be released from the hospital Wednesday morning." Without saying goodbye, she hangs up. Kim is right; I know he has been hiding this from me and others.

The weather on the morning of Wednesday, August 24, is lovely. I walk outside and sit in a quiet, shaded area of our backyard. I close my eyes to listen to the birds and the low rumble of cars driving down Raymond Avenue. The heat of a new summer day warms my cheeks and my tired bones. The ringing of the telephone breaks into my thoughts.

It's Richard. "Hi, Mom, bad news. My surgeon's assistant called early this morning, and they want me back in the hospital today so they can remove the other thyroid lobe. Upon further examination of the lobe that was removed, they found abnormal cell activity equating to very active cancer cells."

I feel lost and alone. What is happening? How could he be okay one moment and terrible the next? Why? I sit in my familiar green kitchen chair, trying to rationalize all of this.

Richard fills me in on his condition. "There are five primary types of thyroid cancer. My tumor growth has been rapid—that does not mean it falls under anaplastic thyroid cancer per se, but its growth rate does concern the doctors."

I interrupt, saying, "Why did you single out this one of the five types?"

Richard hesitates. "It's the rarest type, and the worst. It can start from benign thyroid tumors, which are what they thought I had. Most people, after being diagnosed with it, rarely live beyond five to six months."

I begin to tear up. "What are you telling me, Richard?"

"It's rare and not likely. We just don't know. I am hoping it's one of the other types. Specifically, I am hoping for papillary or follicular thyroid cancer. Those have much higher survival rates. If it is one of those types, I will undergo radioactive iodine therapy—it's very effective."

Finding my footing, I project my concern. "Richard, how are you holding up to all this?"

"Mom," Richard says somberly, "I lost my best friend last year in a plane crash, only a few days after his fortieth birthday. I've climbed out of living in my car and cheap motels and experienced a life far beyond anything I could have imagined while I was growing up in Pasadena. I've taken a company public. If it is time for me to go, I am humbly ready."

I am silent, having no thoughts to share, no words of comfort. After we end our call, I sit in the kitchen holding the handset, in a trance.

Richard's call before his emergency second operation gives me pause. But I will not lose my faith. His condition is uncertain—the spectrum of options he presented ranges from follow-up radiation treatment to a limited time left to live—yet he faces it with dignity and a clear understanding of his responsibilities. From the age of three, when he suggested Aunt June stand on the chair to clean the top of the sliding glass door, he has recognized patterns in life. I know he is an old soul.

I return to a safe space of mindfulness and tranquility—I need to prepare for battle. A battle against Richard's cancer. The tea ceremony and consumption of the matcha tea clears my thoughts and my anxieties. I look up and ask, "Is this his last journey? Was saving my life his final test?" I cry gentle tears of hope—a hope that calls forth the spiritual healing power that will keep me from losing my mystical child to his battle with cancer.

16

One Wish and Tome's Gift

"I have a dream that my four little children will one day live in a nation where they will not be judged by the color of their skin but by the content of their character." These are the words of Dr. Martin Luther King, extracted from his "I Have a Dream" speech, presented at the March on Washington, DC, in 1963. My one wish mirrors his: "I have a dream that my children will one day live in a nation where they will not be judged by their heritage, and that the world will find a balanced humanity in which there exists an authentic reciprocity of respect and friendship."

The five years after Richard is treated for thyroid cancer have become a blurred memory. Luckily, the cancer does not return. In the summer of 2000, six years after Richard's diagnosis, I move Set-chan into an independent care facility, Keiro. After eight years of caring for him and forty-five years of living on Raymond Avenue, I acknowledge it is too much to manage on my own. As I depart from my first visit to Set-chan in his new home, I turn and see in his eyes loneliness, despair, and betrayal.

In the fall of 2000, I move into a small condo a few blocks south of Colorado Boulevard in Pasadena, California. After the move, I am lost. Nothing is familiar. There are no trees that bear fruit, no garden to tend, and no memories of my children growing up. I have compressed my life into a neat and tidy package that foreshadows a seasonal change and impending closure. The chill of the fall winds reminds me of our efforts to establish our life after we were imprisoned at Gila River. Only this time, I am alone.

*   *   *

On November 25, 2002, Set-chan and I celebrate our six-tieth anniversary at the Keiro facility. Surrounded by staff members, other patients, and a few family members, we toast with ginger ale in paper cups. The celebration is oddly similar to our wedding day, when a few friends and family toasted our union with paper cups filled with warm tea. We agree that our compatibility over the past sixty years together reflects our *juunishi* animals, Set-chan a rabbit and me a dog. Sitting in his wheelchair, body withered by old age and his stroke, Set-chan slowly places his quivering left hand on mine and mumbles, "Thank you, Tome .... You will always be my bride. There could never be anyone else."

Two weeks later, on December 5, 2002, Set-chan closes his eyes and leaves behind his empty physical shell. I am prepared, but not ready. After his funeral service I sit alone in the stark-white living room of my newer condo. In putting him in the rest home, did I fail my *ikigai*?

During our life together, we endured a world war, found ourselves incarcerated without due process in a country where we were both citizens, raised five kids, and stayed together during his crippling auto accident and recent debil-itating stroke, all while holding hope that someday our children would not have to fight the intense racial discrimi-nation we faced as visual enemies and outcasts of America. I wonder if his spirit will return to his hometown, Hiroshima, to join his childhood friends and relatives.

The thought of Hiroshima brings to mind the story of Sadako Sasaki, a victim of the atomic bomb dropped on the city on August 6, 1945. This story brings hope for his peace in the afterlife. Unlike Set-chan, who was not present when the bomb was dropped and passed away at the age of eighty-eight, Sadako and many of Set-chan's friends had their lives cut short. Their collective stories are tragic, but Sadako's story leaves a powerful memory and a key message from these victims to share with everyone else.

There are several versions of Sadako's life story, but I haven't seen one that includes her older brother, Masahiro Sasaki. Both Masahiro and his younger sister, Sadako, were living in Hiroshima at the time of the atomic bomb blast. The bomb's destructive results and the resulting human death toll were ghastly. But from the ruins left behind by its explosive power rose Sadako's story of courage and humanity. Literally emerging from the rubble, amid screams of pain and agony and clumps of human flesh scattered around them, Masahiro and Sadako found themselves survivors of the most power-ful weapon of war ever deployed. Even the subsequent black rain, resembling liquid tar, that fell on their tiny bodies could not destroy them.

But the aftermath of the radiation exposure targeted Sadako, and she was plagued with leukemia. Like me, she was an athlete and wanted to run on her school's racing team. At eleven years old she faced a prolonged hospital stay—unless, by some miracle, her wish was granted and she could return to school and run competitively. A friend, Chizuko, visited Sadako in the hospital. Chizuko told Sadako about a legend that says if someone folds one thousand cranes, their wish will be granted. From that point forward, Sadako focused on folding one thousand cranes so that she could earn her one wish to compete as a runner in school. She completed the task of folding one thousand cranes.

On the morning of October 25, 1955, at the age of twelve, her family and friends gathered around her. After quietly thanking them all, she closed her eyes forever. I do believe that on her passing she was granted her wish to run competitively for her school. Her life story is memorialized in a statue for the children of the atomic bomb at the Peace Memorial Park in Hiroshima.

Maybe Set-chan is there too. I hope he is visiting and laughing with his relatives and old friends. I smile, imagining Set-chan living in eternity, which prompts me to wonder about mine. There are patterns in life that become more obvious as our time nears its end. In this twilight moment of my life, three questions arise.

"Who am I?"

Without hesitation I answer, "I am a wife, a mother, and a lifelong learner."

My bookcase has always been a good friend. I stop and stare at it. The rickety pressboard bookcase slants to the right. Four shelves of books wait for any sudden movement to spew their contents across the small room. Many Southern California earthquakes have failed to accomplish this feat.

The books are pressed tightly against each other, reinforcing the structural sturdiness of the dusty, chestnut-brown, veneered bookcase. Like a tightly knit family, together the books prove too strong to succumb to any catastrophes.

My bookcase contains a family possessed of knowledge constructed from many trips to Vroman's Bookstore. I muse over the multicolored jackets of books on topics ranging from law to foreign languages, Japanese woodblock art, home medical treatments, American and Japanese history (especially about World War I and World War II), and novels about racial challenges, like *The Color Purple* or *Roots*. Collecting and reading books has provided a safe way for me to acquire knowledge and has compensated for the post-high school studies I was denied due to being incarcerated during the war.

One enormous picture book, occupying the right corner of my makeshift desk, features the history of Japanese woodblock prints. I have been studying late-1800s, Meiji-era Japanese woodblock artists and have found two, Mizuno Toshikata and Tsukioka Yoshitoshi, who most likely produced my prized prints that were saved from destruction during World War II.

On my small nightstand rests the book *Paris 1919: Six Months That Changed The World*, written by Margaret MacMillan and published in 2003. It has several long, narrow bookmarks protruding from its bound pages. Last year, during one of our long telephone calls, I shared with Richard my thoughts about its contents. I hope what I have learned, and how I have learned it, have transferred to my children as a simple habit. I hope my dedication to my children translates into their commitment to living a better life.

"Why was I incarcerated in 1942?"

Without hesitation I answer, "Reason may have been trumped by fear and possibly greed." Two items stand out: the Munson Report and the Treaty of Versailles.

The Munson Report

I first read about the Munson report in *Years of Infamy*, written by Michi Nishiura in 1996. It sits on the third shelf of my bookcase. It caught my attention at Vroman's Bookstore because her name sounded familiar, and several weeks later I bought it. After reading it, I realize Michi was incarcerated with me at the Gila River Camp. She shares the following information with me and her other readers:

> *Prior to the declaration of war on Japan, the State Department had made war preparations by investigating the possibility of relocating the Japanese Americans on the West Coast of the United States. Special agent Curtis Munson was ordered by the State Department to conduct a study on the Japanese Americans located on the West Coast.*

In late fall of 1941, Munson delivers his report to President Roosevelt. Munson's report clearly states there is no need for military action for a mass incarceration and concludes there will not be an armed uprising of the local Japanese. The report suggests they are loyal to the United States and uphold a stable, honorable, and disciplined family life. The report continues with comments indicating that the Japanese display a pathetic eagerness to be Americans.

Three months after Munson submits his report, United States Executive Order 9066 is signed and shortly thereafter implemented. The executive order calls for the forceful relocation and incarceration of Japanese living on the West Coast. In total, there are ten relocation camps, also referred to as internment camps, located in California, Arizona, Colorado, Idaho, Arkansas, Utah, and Wyoming. The largest population is held at Tule Lake in California. This camp is the troubled camp, which houses what might be considered disruptive Japanese.

My opinion of the impact of Munson's report: zero.

The Paris Peace Conference and the Treaty of Versailles

Glancing back at my nightstand, I see *Paris 1919* and decide to revisit it.

Chapter 23 exposes the same concerns Ojiichan's father expressed in 1924. He wanted Ojiichan to return to Japan after his last tour aboard the *Explorer*. He suggested that America had humiliated Japan and it was time to come home. At the Paris Peace Conference, two experienced diplomats—Baron Nobuaki Makino, who had been foreign minister, and Viscount Sutemi Chinda, who was ambassador to Great Britain—had secured the inclusion, by League majority vote, of a racial-equality paragraph into the Treaty of Versailles. One person stood in its way. Through an obscure unanimous voting rule, President Woodrow Wilson killed its entry into the treaty. This stoppage clearly inferred that the Japanese race was inferior to those in the West. Ironically in 1920, President Woodrow Wilson was awarded the Nobel Peace Prize for his work at the Paris Peace Conference. This was followed by another blow when the United States ruled Japanese racially unfit to be naturalized citizens by passage of the Immigration Act of 1924. It also banned any further immigration from Japan.

My opinion of the impact of excluding the racial-equity paragraph from the 1919 Treaty of Versailles and the Immigration Act of 1924: high for the world and for me.

I still don't have a complete answer to my question: "Why was I incarcerated in 1942?" Most likely, I never will. What I will remember is how Dr. Martin Luther King Jr., in the final words of his 1963 "I Have a Dream" speech, embodied my feelings as I departed my World War II prison in Gila River, Arizona: "Free at last. Free at last. Thank God Almighty, we are free at last."

"Is a balanced humanity possible?"

Without hesitation I answer, "Yes, I have witnessed it and experienced it."

I look back at Richard's marriage to and divorce from Kim. They tried hard to figure it out, but long hours and stress created a barrier they couldn't breach. I am sad to see him alone. Richard formed a close relationship with Kim's dad, Dusty; their friendship was strengthened

Richard and Dusty—Thanksgiving family dinner. CMDR (retired) Raleigh E. "Dusty" Rhodes, Navy fighter pilot (WWII and Korean War). Third flight leader for the Navy Blue Angels. Inducted into American Combat Airman Hall of Fame. His story: *From POW to Blue Angel.*

by their common love of flying. Richard described piloting his father-in-law through airspace above the beaches of Northern California as rich stories of the war echoed inside the cockpit.

I love sitting at the makeshift desk in my bedroom, reading Richard's letters. One letter starts with Dusty reliving his days climbing and diving in his Grumman Wildcat fighter plane above the Haleakala volcano on Maui, Hawaii, during World War II. His ship, the USS *Enterprise*, with its rolling landing deck, waited just a short distance away. There, frozen in time, Dusty is captured in the disciplined freedom of a Navy fighter pilot in wartime conditions; his eyes would soon be focused on enemies in the sky. He is proud to have served as a member of Jimmy Flatley's Grim Reaper Navy fighter pilot team.

During one of our telephone conversations, Richard shares these thoughts: "Mom, sometimes when I fly with Dusty, in the deafening silence of the cockpit, I can hear his silent screams of agony. Dusty's calm demeanor masks the deep torment he is holding at bay. He never talks in detail about the war battles or his flight missions. He is vague about his experience as a prisoner of war in the Japanese war camps, but the conditions were clearly brutal. He mentions that he respects the Japanese fighter pilots—they were both warriors, fighting for what they believed was right, and against what was wrong in the world."

Richard standing in front of his airplane

When I learn of Dusty's years in captivity, tortured in Japanese prisoner-of-war camps, and his sense of a balanced humanity, I develop a deep admiration for him. One example of his decency is brought to my attention when Richard mentions he has seen a letter that Dusty wrote in 1946 in support of one of his Japanese captors, Master Sergeant Keioshi Iida of the Japanese Imperial Army. In the letter, Dusty specifically notes that Master Sergeant Iida should not be prosecuted as a war criminal.

As I walk to the kitchen and stand over the kitchen sink, I envision Richard and Dusty slicing through space in my son's airplane above the beaches of Northern California. The waves roll below them, just as they did in the Pacific Ocean, battering Dusty after he was shot down during the Battle of the Santa Cruz Islands. To me, this is an iconic scene: two pilots, a young Japanese American private pilot and a former World War II US Navy fighter pilot, occupying the same cockpit, some sixty years later. A spark of pride lifts my eyes, and I look out my kitchen window and glimpse clear skies and hope. Richard's letters and life are proof that a balanced humanity is possible. I am so relieved and gratified to see this in him.

I am reminded of my high school friend, Lois Norman. Her regal appearance did not mask her true friendship with me, the Jap girl. The last time I saw Lois was in 1942, through the window of a train taking me away to be incarcerated for the duration of the war. Her tears as she watched me depart were real, and I miss our friendship . . . lost to the specter of war.

After reflecting on these three questions, I return to Sadako's story of the one thousand cranes. Like her, I have one wish. Every Christmas after the war, we receive hundreds of Christmas cards, but never as many as one thousand. I believe if we receive one thousand Christmas cards in any one year, it will be like the one thousand cranes in Sadako's story, and I will be granted my one wish.

I see friends leaving, and I see family growing old and departing. I realize my time is coming to an end. It's strange to see our lives as history and our future coming at us with ferocious speed. I will miss my early-morning walks, chats on the telephone, memories of my youth, and the warmth of human touch. I wonder, will my emotions survive the transition? Or do we lose what makes us appear real to ourselves? The human element is so strange when viewed close to departure.

*　*　*

From my journal (March 14, 2004):
It's now fourteen months after Set-chan passed, and my pain has increased. I question why I can't shake this throbbing inside me. No doctor for me. I turn to my trusty medical books, which have diagnosed my kids' and foster parents' many ailments. No answers appear, and I grasp the reality that old age, a life of hardship, and stress have robbed me of future time here.

It's March 14 and life's colors have changed. I no longer see the different shades. It is this starkness that signals a change in my heart and not in my eyes. My tired bones and muscles welcome a hot cup of tea and the low tones of a koto playing in the background. The sound of June Kuramoto and the band Hiroshima brings me joy. Two songs linger: "Thousand Cranes" and "One Wish." I shuffle between rooms, wanting the sunlight to greet me. I slowly dress and find myself sitting on a bench outside my condo. Pasadena in March is typically cool in the late mornings as we await the start of spring. The swaying of new leaves hints of warm summer breezes months away. This is my last journal entry as I can no longer hold a pen steady—the pain is constant and everywhere in my body.

A week passes. Today is March 20—I have turned eighty-two. I miss my kids, I miss the comfort of sharing stories with my sisters, and I miss the days when moving was not such a chore. I miss my foster parents. Remembering them, I become absorbed in memories of my early childhood experience of abandonment and wonder how I became so fearless and understood so much at such an early age. Over my lifetime of quietly observing many evening horizons, my moist, aging eyes absorbing the orange-and-pink rays of countless sunsets, the same question has repeatedly come back to me: "Why was I the only child of nine to be given away?" That is quickly followed by another question: "Is my life worth anything?" It is haunting, knowing that

Tome performing tea ceremony

getting invited somewhere does not necessarily mean you belong.

I have been in pain for most of my life, but recently it is beyond bearable. If I could, if I were able, I would like to perform one last tea ceremony. One more to prepare me for what lies ahead. Ojiichan mentioned that samurai would perform a tea ceremony before and after battle. I know it would be proper now as I enter a battle for my life.

Today my pain is replaced with an air of hope and happiness. I am in the hospital, and next to me, collecting dust, is a solitary birthday card. The sight of that one card brings a smile to my face. I close my eyes, trying to escape the fatigue in my body. My nephew, Ken, and others who have passed reach out to me. Surrounding me are the one thousand Christmas cards scattered throughout my home on Raymond Avenue. I glide among these trophies of my life, reminded of my World War II prison friends. These one thousand Christmas cards form a bridge beyond this moment.

* * *

It's the morning of March 28. Joyfully, I run across open fields in Southern California. Giggling, I sprint toward the schoolyard fence and gently fall to my knees. I struggle to stand up and take one long, deep breath. The fresh farmland air fills my nostrils with the tingling scents of fresh flowers. My life is witnessed through the sparkling eyes of a young Jap girl standing in an open field, waving goodbye and whispering, "My name is Tome. Please never forget me."

I know my time is near. My physical body struggles to let go. I am no longer lost or in pain. When I was forty, Richard kept me here. Now, I am eighty-two, and he is here to let me go. Last night, his solitary vigil helped bridge my path to eternity. This morning the shadowy figure of the *Shinigami* at the foot of my bed holds a flickering candle.

The *Shinigami* speaks to me. "Tome, I do not have the power to decide who lives and who dies. When your candle goes out, it is time."

I am proud to have been the wife of Set-chan for sixty years. It has been an honor to be the mother of my children. Each has their own unique story of success. My *ikigai* gifted them the opportunity to create a balanced humanity within their respective lives. Clinging to my final moments, I now understand why I was the only child of nine to be given away. I was granted a better life, reared as an only child and adopted into a samurai family. My siblings suffered from a lack of food, clothing, and education. I was gifted all these things. My siblings fought to be noticed, while I was gifted unrivaled attention. Such as now, when others who have passed before me reach out with welcome. My flickering candle turns cold. The merit of being an old soul marks this as my final journey. Taunting the *Shinigami*, I believe dreams and stories that are passed on, generation to generation, can live forever.

I hear a whisper coming from behind me. "My name is Tome. Please never forget me."

The young Jap girl steps forward. We stand together, side by side.

"Tome, you have shown great courage in completing and being true to your *ikigai*. Your tears reflect the passage of Bushido to your children. You are worthy."

Our laughter eternally binds us. As we smile and hold hands, I momentarily bend down to leave behind a small box that contains not just Bushido artifacts, but the soul of my *ikigai*. The gifts wrapped in this box include one envelope filled with my typed memoir notes, my tea set, and my ikebana *kenzan*.

The Jap girl lifts me up and smiles. Together we step across the threshold of a bright orange *torii* gate and enter an orchard of dormant cherry trees. Together we shed our physical presence as we glide over a beautiful pink blanket of fallen Sakura. My spirit intertwines with the purity and dignity of the young Jap girl as we become one. Our metamorphosis opens the door for my one wish to be granted: that the world may one day find a balanced humanity—an authentic reciprocity of respect and friendship—by repairing its fractures with lines of healing gold, discovering beauty and dignity within its imperfect pieces: *Kintsugi*.

Epilogue

One Generation Away

In the Japanese culture, the number four is considered ominous or bad luck because it is pronounced the same way as the word for death. In the Japanese culture, it is believed you should avoid things that are made of four parts. In the Japanese culture, hospitals and hotels sometimes skip the number four when labeling a room or a floor. In the Japanese culture, it is believed you should toss aside anything made up of four elements. But in life, certain things cannot be avoided, skipped, or tossed aside—they must be dealt with, as I have done in my life. My name is Richard, and I am the fourth child of Tome, standing one generation away.

I can still hear Mom's voice: *Never give up.* When I was struggling, she supported me, saying, "Richard, you may be just a late bloomer.... Keep at it and it will happen." She transformed how I define success in my life—not as a final result, but the completion of a journey, never giving up in the face of difficulties encountered along the way.

After surviving cancer and multiple operations to rebuild my neck, on March 28, 2004, when we were thirty years apart in age, I inherited her handwritten journals and a box containing a tea set, an envelope with her typed memoir notes, and a *kenzan*. Inspired by her spirit and her belief in me, I am fulfilling a promise I made on the day before she passed away, March 27, 2004, to author her story, *American Jap Girl*. The goal is not publication alone, but to share a compelling story of growth, relentless effort, joy, and overcoming all the life challenges that added up to her *ikigai*. This was her lived odyssey. She envisioned a much better one for me.

It was twelve years ago that I read Mom's eulogy here at Mountain View Mortuary in Altadena, California, where both Dad and Mom were cremated. I have come to the mortuary today to reflect upon her gifts to me: her journals, her memoir notes, our countless conversations, and her *ikigai*.

The mortuary is a few blocks from my high school, where I attended a ceremony inducting me into the John Muir High School Hall of Fame, coming full circle from the 1947 celebration for Jackie Robinson in our old neighborhood near Pepper Street, which Mom described earlier. We are both graduates of John Muir High School, and we are both members of the Hall of Fame. At the ceremony,

Congressperson Judy Chu and Richard

Congressperson Judy Chu awarded me a Congressional Certificate of Recognition, and my picture now graces the same wall where his picture hangs.

I had the opportunity to chat with Jackie Robinson's nephew, Ed Robinson, who accepted the award for his dad. Ed's dad was Mack Robinson, the older and often-forgotten brother of Jackie Robinson, who took part in the 1936 Olympics in Berlin. Mack captured a silver medal, losing to Jesse Owens by four-tenths of a second in the two-hundred-meter dash. Mack's final resting spot is also here in Altadena.

As I look at the grass surrounding the mortuary, I remember Mom's stories, her lessons, and her wisdom. My childhood experiences pushed me outside my comfort zone at an early age. Today, I hope that the pages from her memoirs will bring closure to one powerful moment in particular that irrevocably changed my life.

I stare down Raymond Avenue and visualize our old house several blocks away. That house owns forty-five years of our lives. I drop my head, absorbing its innocence and its pain, and then open my eyes and look up. Hunting for the wild parrots that once roamed the tall palm trees, I call out and receive no reply. I am greeted by an empty, pale-blue sky. I gasp for air and find calm by our cyclone fence, which now outlines the perimeter of our old house. The shadows cast by its mesh are reminiscent of the many bars on our windows and doors, which defined my years of confinement. I forfeited freedom for an illusory safety. But without this illusion, fear might have crowded out my hopes and dreams.

I remember my childhood days and flash on this quote: "Poverty gives rise to a desire for change." My economic poverty drove the desire for change deep into my character. So deep, it took the central place in my life, pushing away many people I loved. The resurrected whisper of my "poverty voice" brings a chill. I grit my teeth, knowing I need to face my lifelong companion and destroy it. My character will not allow it to control me.

In the distance, a sullen-looking gentleman is staring at a burial site. He shifts his attention to me and, with a purposeful stride, begins walking in my direction, holding his gaze steadily on me. As he draws closer, his dark demeanor and dark features are illuminated by direct sunlight, softening his facial lines. His green eyes meet mine.

"Are you here to meet someone?" he calls out.

"No . . . just reflecting on my mom and dad."

He hesitates and then says, "I work here; maybe I know them. What are their names?"

"Tome and Setsuji Okumoto," I say cautiously.

His surly gaze is replaced by a puzzled look. "I have never heard the name Tome before . . . . How do you spell it?"

"T-O-M-E," I quickly blurt out.

"How odd, why would anyone name a child that? That's the word for a book, a large scholarly work. And why pronounce it that way? It should be pronounced 'tohm.'"

He walks away, shaking his head from side to side. I think for a moment. Tome (toh-meh) means *stop* in Japanese—what is so odd about that?

A soft whisper floats behind me. "My name is Tome." I turn around, expecting to see Mom. Then the whisper floats down from above. "My name is Tome. Please never forget me."

I say it aloud. "Tome. Tohm?"

As I consider the difference in pronunciation, I am hit with the obvious. Her name, and the English word for a large, scholarly book—a member of a much larger body of knowledge and wisdom—are spelled the same. There are no coincidences in life, just unrecognized patterns. This knowledge is ingrained in me from countless conversations with Mom. I stand motionless, dumbfounded. After a slight hesitation, I cautiously accept the truth.

Mom's life and *ikigai* resembled a large, scholarly book, part of a universal collection. This collection is filled with the souls of all mothers who have silently given their lives for their children. She was not just my mom; she was everyone's mom. Her dreams and sacrifices were those of every mother—rich or poor, white, Black, or yellow—who wants more for her children, who wants her children to be kind and their lives to be wonderful.

Never acknowledging her many sacrifices, Mom always questioned, "Is my life worth anything?" To me, her value and destiny were never in question. She shared her common sense, her rational thinking, her knowledge, her ability to see and touch life as well as death, her belief in the American dream, and her belief in me.

I begin to understand her lost years, her toil, and her dignity. From between the pages of one of the journals I am carrying, a letter—its paper an off-brown color—falls out and onto the ground. On the back side, written in her handwriting, is a date: October 15, 1990. The letter is from the White House in Washington, DC.

A monetary sum and words alone cannot restore
lost years and painful memories; neither can they

fully convey our Nation's resolve to rectify injustice and to uphold the rights of individuals. We can never fully right the wrongs of the past. But we can take a clear stand for justice and recognize that serious injustices were done to Japanese Americans during World War II.

In enacting a law calling for restitution and offering a sincere apology, your fellow Americans have, in a very real sense, renewed their traditional commitment to the ideals of freedom, equality, and justice. You and your family have our best wishes for the future.

Sincerely,
George H. W. Bush
President of the United States

This letter exposes how Mom was silenced. This letter confirms her worth as an American. Thank you, President Bush, for the apology and for reminding Mom that she is an American. Thank you, President Ronald Reagan, for signing the Civil Liberties Act of 1988, which made this happen. Thank you, Linda Gordon and Gary Okihiro, for publishing Dorothea Lange's censored images of life in the Japanese American war camps, enabling me to visualize those times. I carefully place the letter back into the journal and close it.

Mom's journals captured her thoughts, her ideals, her hopes and dreams, her sadness and happiness. I have looked at them hundreds of times. I have read them many, many times. As I lay them down, the wind ruffles the leaves of one of the journals and opens it to a page for me to read.

Mom survived her older sister Fumi, the family's fourth daughter. Upon Fumi's death, Mom assumed and embraced Fumi's position in the family.

When I glance away from that page, that same warm breeze is working its way through the high palm trees, which are subtly swaying to a muffled rhythm. This rhythm conjures up an old friend—my best friend, Russ Fisher. Together we skied treacherous mountains, hiked in valleys of waving grass, and traveled to my ancestral home. Like Mom, Russ was knowing and peaceful. I never understood how he maintained his reassuring demeanor throughout our friendship.

Now, he stands by me, grinning his familiar grin. "Well, are you going to open the envelope or not?" Coaxing me, as he always did, to move beyond my fear.

I smile back, as I always have, my way of thanking Russ for being my best friend.

My cell phone buzzes and I excuse myself to answer it.

A strong, determined voice with an Australian accent asks, "When are you coming back to the car?" The question is quickly repeated, and I smile.

The sound of Stefanie's voice evokes an image of an innocent four-year-old child vacating her scarred, war-torn homeland in Cologne, Germany. Embarking upon her new life in the land down under, Stefanie fought loneliness through endless days exploring the beaches north of Sydney, Australia. As she looked out over the ocean from Dee Why

Headland, she wished to find herself living beyond the horizon. It was there that she saw what could be and what must be if she were to find herself—to find home.

Never abandoning her dreams of coming to America, Stefanie followed a path that led her to become an accidental contestant, representing her country as Miss Australia, at the 1969 Miss World competition, held at the Royal Albert Hall in London. She celebrated her twenty-first birthday at the competition, and then traveled to vacation destinations in Japan, Southeast Asia, and the Hawaiian Islands, as well as across Europe. While looking for home, Stefanie met and shook hands with Philip Mountbatten, the Duke of Edinburgh, was engaged to the president of the Seychelles, and dated the future prime minister of Australia.

Eventually her travels delivered her to her chosen destination, America. In a land that promises opportunity, the shy and lonely little girl inside Stefanie found home. And she found me, a shy and lonely Jap boy from a bad neighborhood.

Now, she is wondering when I am coming back to her.

"Soon," I whisper. "I will be there soon."

I look over to Russ, ready to ask him if he wants to come home and have dinner with Stefanie and me. We have recently settled into our new home in Newport Beach. But Russ is no longer on the grassy spot where he was standing. Where is he? My smile saddens as I am reminded that twenty years ago, on June 13, Russ died with his father in a plane crash. That day was also a sad one for Ojiichan, for June 13 marks the anniversary of the death of Musashi Miyamoto, the greatest samurai. I close my eyes, realizing

Russ will not return . . . until perhaps one day when I need him again.

"Thank you, Russ. Soon."

I draw from my shirt pocket an old, yellowing envelope, one of three gifts from Mom. I have come here to read a few typed pages from her memoir notes, kept in this envelope. It is fitting that I read them here, in close proximity to our home of forty-five years. I carefully open the envelope and readjust the stack of neatly folded and sorted papers. There, on the first page, is my name. I begin to read aloud, placing my hand over my mouth to keep from voicing my thoughts, which are screaming with pain and fear. I am again that ten-year-old boy in Pasadena, reliving a terrifying moment.

* * *

Sitting in our living room at the Raymond Avenue house, I hear Mom's liminal voice calling out for help. I am not sure where it came from. But then I hear it again—it sounds like it came from the back porch. I get up from the couch and cautiously walk toward it. No one is there. The back door has a window, and when I look through it, I notice the side door to the garage is slightly ajar and light is spilling out onto the concrete path outside the entry. I go out the back door and walk down the steps to the garage. When I reach the side door, I begin to shiver, although I am not cold. I am not sure what lies ahead, but I am scared. I need to go inside to see why the light is on. I slowly open the weather-faded side door and enter. It is dimly lit inside, yet I clearly understand the situation, the danger.

Piercing the darkness that fills the garage is a lighted tunnel that guides me to Mom, who is standing on a kitchen chair, a rough braided rope around her neck. Without hesitation I run to her. Standing in front of her, I look up. Mom towers above me, and I see only her falling tears—a blinding rain, depositing moist droplets that scatter across the green vinyl of the chair. Her feet, wearing her off-white, soft-soled work shoes, are stretched out and gripping the seat cushion. Her shoes squeak, alerting me that she is sliding off the end of the chair. For a brief moment, she looks down; her eyes are vacant. They scare me and haunt me. She is silent. Why can I hear her screaming when there is no sound?

Instinctively I leap forward and hold her as tight as I can. For the longest moments of my short life, I hold her. My strength drains and my arms spasm and twitch violently. Sweat breaks out on my forehead, emphasizing the futility of my feverish fight. The pain in my muscles gives way to a mind-numbing fear. My youth is no match.

But I cannot and will not let go.

My shirt absorbs her tears, which renew my arm strength. My triple-cuffed blue jeans tightening around my weakening legs, I close my eyes to meet the darkness. In the depth of the blackness, my pounding heart blocks out the world. There is no time to run for help, there is no time to cry, there is only time to react.

"Please, God, please, do not let her slip away," I pray, over and over.

I hold tight to her, hoping I will not lose her.

I cry out my fear and hope.

I cry out as loudly as I can.

And I promise God, again and again, "I will not let go . . . . I will not leave her."

From Tome's memoirs (no date):
My son Richard found me in the garage with a rope made into a noose that I had thrown over a beam. He threw himself around my waist and cried, "No, Mommy, no!" I realized what a horrible thing I was about to do to this innocent child who means so much to me.

The expression on Mom's face transforms from anguish and fear to shame and remorse. Color returns to her cheeks. The emptiness in her eyes is replaced by a dull sheen of sadness. She finds strength, and her lips curve into a slow smile that reflects a newfound peace. She stops crying, steps down from the chair, and wraps her arms around me. In that garage in Pasadena, only the two of us, mother and son, live that moment. Only the two of us are judged. Only we know that it is a turning point in our lives, and only we can understand the power that pulled her back from the threshold of death.

*   *   *

What drove Mom to this point?

Was it fear or desperation?

Was it the devastating accident that had recently crippled her husband, or was it the recent loss of her second foster father, Father Kawakita, tinging her smile with sadness? Could it have been the shallow pit she had descended into, knowing her foster mother had taken her own life four years earlier to avoid being a burden to the family? Could it have been her failure to take care of her children and thus fulfill her *ikigai*?

Whatever her reasons, after she got down from that chair, Mom held me so tight, I knew she did not want me to slip away.

But I *had* slipped away.

At the age of ten, my childhood innocence was lost forever, and my freedom went with it. Now, I realize that my physically holding her was not what stopped Mom from killing herself. Rather, it was the meaning and purpose she found when she saw me. When she stood at the precipice of life and death, the power of motherhood and her *ikigai* gave her strength to choose life and delay the inevitable fate of death. She rediscovered the soul of a three-year-old girl who had once walked into her aunt's farmhouse and declared her position in life. This miracle moment, pivotal in my life and our family's, transformed my childhood from a journey of searching into a journey of purpose and hope.

Mom once told me, "We may not see miracles coming at us or upon us." I clearly missed it then, but I appreciate it now. For many years I thought that memory was a bad dream or a nightmare of my youth. I now know her plea for help was real and her confrontation with mortality transformed her. When Mom stepped down from her perch, I thought I had saved her life. I was wrong. Mom saved my life and accepted the power of her *ikigai*.

Released from my childhood nightmares and insomnia, released from the responsibility for my actions that day, I find my freedom. Understanding this, I see Mom's freedom.

In her own voice, she has told the story of her life: her dreams, her ideals, and her losses. In her own voice, she conveyed her knowledge and her wisdom with both logic and joy. She fulfilled the promise, her *ikigai*, to take care of us, her children. Her work—to provide a safe place for our souls to grow and learn—was one of many important gifts she gave us.

As I walk toward my car, I take a deep breath, and the image of the street I traveled down in my youth begins to dim. Tears form as I see Dad walking to the street to wish me well and wave goodbye. Mom is holding back by the front door of our old house. There she stands, smiling from the weather-beaten front porch. Her presence leads me to glance back at her memoirs and reread the open page in disbelief.

I turn my head slowly and see Dad smiling, almost grinning. Mom looks peaceful, compassionate, and knowing. I stand petrified as she motions to me and then gracefully reveals her fate, whispering, "Like you always told me, we have no secrets, Richard."

Mom had the courage to fend off the physical devastation of polio, found her soul within an abandoned three-year-old child, kept her spirits up during her incarceration in the World War II Japanese American war camps, and at the age of forty dealt with the loss of her foster parents and crippling of her husband. She faced the daunting task of raising her children on her own, fighting her way through loneliness, despair, and poverty, and managed to help send several kids to college. She held on to the responsibilities of parenting in the face of enormous obstacles and tirades from a husband driven out of his mind by years of pain and drugs. She understood how demeaning it was to give up her office job in downtown Los Angeles and return to domestic work cleaning homes, but she did so with integrity to ensure the survival of her family.

In the midst of battling her demons of abandonment, she still gave to others. Her loyalty—a quality that is seemingly lost to society today—led her to care, at the age of seventy, for her stroke-inflicted husband for more than eight years. She projected a magical aura of kindness and compassion that enabled her to find friends in whatever walk of life she found herself, while constantly questioning, "Is my life worth anything?" Mom was not someone who could be avoided, skipped, or tossed aside—she was someone to be reckoned with. She was a fourth child who extended her dreams to one generation away.

I am that one generation away. I am the benefactor of her joy in life, her *ikigai*. This gift enabled me, a young, insecure Jap boy from humble roots—who is not a genius, who lacks any special talents or skills, who is not the most outgoing or good-looking, who sometimes questions his self-worth—to attend good schools of higher education and create an amazing life.

Over her lifetime and mine, Mom's *ikigai* gift has transformed me. In 1974, during my first job search after graduating from SJSU, Mom taught me *gambari*. Her lessons awakened my tenacity and determination.

During the first seven months of 1986, when I lived on the streets, in my car, or in cheap motels, or couch surfed in friends' homes, Mom and Dad tested my resilience by not allowing me safe passage home. Instead, they helped me endure with patience and dignity what I perceived to be unbearable conditions. They enabled me to internalize *gaman* and grow stronger and wiser.

Of the many traits fundamental to the Bushido code that Mom imparted to me, three stand out: respect and self-worth, discipline, and integrity. She maintained that to earn the respect of others, I needed to respect myself first. I flash on our conversation during the summer of 1973, when she counseled me to achieve personal success by attaining accomplishments and contributing to others. This led me to Silicon Valley C-suite positions and board memberships—specifically, becoming a chief financial officer of a successful technology company and completing an initial public offering (IPO), and becoming a chief executive officer of a technology startup company and selling it for cash the month the dot-com meltdown started.

These Bushido attributes were enhanced by my fifteen-year journey teaching in higher education and contributing to our next generation of leaders. I expanded my contribution to students by launching and becoming the first director of the online MBA program at California State University, Long Beach, and the administrative director for the International Collegiate Business Strategy Competition.

Mom consistently and persistently reminded me of my personal self-worth. To address my discomfort at being a Japanese American male trying to navigate relationships in today's world, she told me the story of Sessue Hayakawa, a Japanese actor in America during the era of silent movies. He played leading-man roles and ascended to stardom, becoming a matinee idol to American women. Yet, he is virtually unknown and ignored today.

When I asked how this related to me, she said, "You are not less than others because you are Japanese American. You and Hayakawa were born on the same day, June 10.... There are patterns in life."

Mom and Dad prepared me to feel worthy enough to marry a former Miss World contestant, Stefanie Meurer.

Mom also directed me to practice certain simple habits—*kaizen*—that added structure and discipline to my life. She encouraged me to study martial arts. I trained under Ken Funakoshi—who was related to the founder of modern karate, Gichin Funakoshi—and attained a black belt in Shotokan karate. Embracing these simple habits also supported my flying skills when I became a licensed private pilot.

In sharing her Bushido lessons, Mom often led by example. Her integrity in remaining loyal to Dad and me was displayed many times. These lessons guided me when I was the CFO of a public company and became a whistleblower under the Sarbanes-Oxley Act. This experience is chronicled in a *Harvard Business Education* case study, "The Midnight Journal Entry."

Beyond her lessons on *gambari*, *gaman*, and Bushido, Mom developed her own tenets, weaving together an impressive fabric of common sense, vision, and the American dream:

- We are ordinary people, but it is what we do with ourselves that can make life exceptional.
- It's never too late to become the person you would like to be.
- Education is the greatest economic equalizer.
- To look beyond what you cannot see, to imagine beyond who you are, to grow beyond your present character, is what marks the soul of a great person. You can be that person.

- You may not see miracles coming at you or upon you. When times are difficult, you must go beyond what you first thought impossible.
- Dreams and lifelong learners live forever.
- Ask yourself, *What can be?* or *What if?* Don't limit yourself to *what is*, and your mind will remain open and alive.
- Many people complain about injustices in our world. Remember, America has given us countless opportunities. My parents came to America to build a better life. Dad and I have talked to you about the American dream. We believe in it. This is what we want you to achieve and what we have prepared you to do. The American dream is still alive. It is up to you to attain it.
- In life, as in origami, understanding patterns empowers you to harness simplicity to achieve beauty and complexity.
- There are no coincidences in life, just unrecognized patterns.

This final tenet, out of all of Mom's sayings and lessons, stands out above the rest. She constantly challenged me to uncover patterns so I could better myself and contribute to others, creating an authentic reciprocity of respect and friendship—what she called a balanced humanity. I hope everyone who reads Tome's story will challenge themselves to find the same.

As I carefully refold the typed memoir notes, I hear a whisper:

Richard, self-respect is the foundation of Bushido.
Your ability to find a balanced humanity tells me

you have found it. With this, you can live Bushido
as your way of life and live world Kintsugi as your
ikigai.

I return the pages to the envelope and place it in my shirt pocket. The meaning of our conversation in 1973, before my departure for my senior year at SJSU, is clearer to me now, more than ever.

As I step into my car, I am greeted by music emanating from my iPhone. I close my eyes, tears rolling down my cheeks, and capture the texture of the rhythm—the music of June Kuramoto and Hiroshima swirling around the interior of my car. I thank June for giving Mom's *koto* a future and bringing so much joy into her life. (In 2024, June received the National Endowment for the Arts National Heritage Fellowship for her lifetime contribution to American culture.)

Beyond the horizon I see an amazing adventure ahead. I look forward to making this journey with Stefanie. I glance into the rearview mirror and see the fading shadows of Dad and Mom, holding each other, smiling, and bowing for the last time. As we drive away, I silently thank them. That once-mystical ten-year-old boy and his father now know Mom was a Japanese American and member of a samurai family, mixing two diverse worlds into her *ikigai*. This is her gift and challenge to everyone, especially for those who sacrifice in silence, extending their dreams to one generation away.

American Jap Girl is the spiritual incarnation of Tome. Her *ikigai* lives on in my heart, on every page of this memoir, and in every reader's heart. We are now one—her story has bound us forever. A whisper floats above me. "My name is Tome. Please never forget me."

Stefanie nods her head in unison with this whisper—is it just coincidence?—and reaches out to hold my hand. "Richard," she says, "I appreciate that today has been difficult. Know that I will always be by your side. I, Stefanie Meurer, believe in you."

I say Stefanie's last name out loud: "Meurer." It sounds like the last name of Mom's best friend in the war camp, Sachiko Miura. Another person who shares that name is Anjin Miura, a rare white person who was granted samurai status. As I reflect on these thoughts, Stefanie caresses my hand. Mom's wish was for me to find someone who would hold my hand, believe in me, and help me believe in myself.

Acknowledging her wish, I continue my journey of perpetuating her gift to me, her *ikigai*, and say, "Stefanie, please, let me tell you a story..."

The End

Acknowledgments

This memoir reflects my gratitude and the love I received from Mom and Dad. Their combined *ikigai* gift paved the way to my amazing life. Although we only had a short time, I thank Grandfather Kawakita for sharing stories of his life, teaching me how to use his abacus, which is sitting in a bookcase behind me, and playing the Japanese games of GO and GOMOKU. I thank my wife Virginia Okumoto, who supported me throughout this sometimes difficult and emotional journey. As the daughter of a Navy rear admiral and former superintendent of the Philadelphia Mint, she brought an amazing family circle into my life. I thank my late wife Stefanie Meurer, a bold and brave Australian whom I lost to breast cancer, for opening my eyes and sharing her bigger and kinder world. And, a special thank you to my late best friend, Russell Roy Fisher. We will always be brothers.

I wish to thank several people who contributed countless hours working with me on this project. One standout couple during this journey was George and Charlene Metzger.

Between reading my work and providing valuable insights, we shared hundreds of telephone hours between California and Tennessee. I also deeply appreciated in-person conversations with Mary (Uyeda) Maruyama, post Mom's passing. She provided a best friend's insight into Mom's school years and the years after they reunited.

I am grateful for my editors, friends, and publishing consultant who supported me by providing a deeper insight into content and structure elements, provided beta reading, reinforced or added to what I understood about my mom, and helped me better understand required publishing and marketing tasks. My developmental editors, copy editor, and proofreader include Jennifer Van Sijll, Nancy Cortelyou, Akiko Tamano, and David Aretha. Friends include Michael Nolan, Dr. Simon Rodan, Joanne Barnett Blodgett, Steve Warren, Carolyn Rogers, and, especially, Ted Ichino. Ted confirmed the information about his father, Sergeant Frank Ichino, regarding his participation in the Battle of the Lost Battalion in WWII as a member of the United States Army's 442 Regimental Combat Team. My publishing consultant, David Wogahn of AuthorImprints, provided much needed insight into this entire process.

I would also like to thank my late father-in-law, CMDR Raleigh "Dusty" Rhodes, for sharing cockpit time, his life as a Navy fighter pilot and Blue Angel flight leader, and insight into his ordeal as a POW during WWII. He was a rare individual who truly lived a balanced humanity.

In closing I want to thank two people who enabled me to write this memoir. Without them, I may not have finished it. This includes Kimberly Rhodes, who cared for me during my bout with thyroid cancer, and Aggie Pagnillo, who acted as my advocate during an emergency second operation to rebuild my neck and save my life. Ironic that two events that nearly killed me left deep scars on the front of my neck.

There are no coincidences in life, just unrecognized patterns.

Examples of Original Field Data

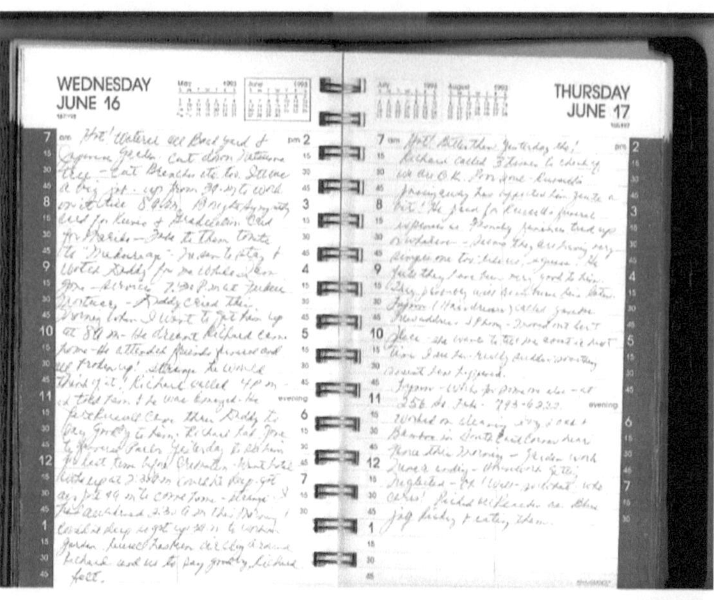

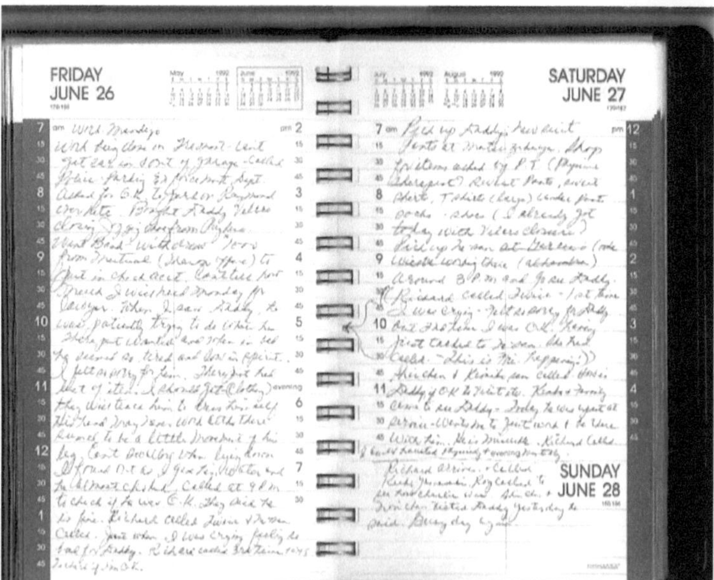

Tome's Handwritten Daily Journals
Four pages from her handwritten daily journals
that span from the 1950s to 2004

Examples of Original Field Data

Tome's Handwritten Cash Journals
Two pages from her handwritten cash journals
that span from the 1960s to 2002

Tome's Typed Memoir Notes

son Richard found me in the garage with a rope thrown over a beam made into
a noose. He threw himself around my waist and cried "No, mommy no!" I
realized what a horrible thing I was about to do these innocent children
who meant so much to me.

One paragraph: Suicide Attempt

The story starts in the summer of 1925. I, Tome at 3 years of age was
going visiting for the first time in my life. Mother with no explanation
dressed me in a clean blue apron-pants. I was so thrilled I could hardly
contain myself. There was a bright red wagon waiting at Aunt Fude and Uncle
Tsuchiyama's. Sisters took turns pulling me around in it. I was having so
much fun I did not notice when father and sisters left. When I realized
they were gone and began searching for them, Aunt Fude gently told me I was
to stay and be their little girl. I strongly refuted it and said they
accidently forgot me and would be back. I stood by the road side and when
I tired I sat hugging my knees. Mulling in my puzzled mind, questioning
and wondering. Biting my lips to avoid crying, and hoping against hope

One paragraph: Abandoned at three years old

There was a need to entertain and keep people occupied so a recreation
program was started. Games, crafts, lessons, and talent shows. One day
while I was ironing and singing my favorite Japanese songs in our small
partitioned room, neighbors , without my knowledge had a recreation head
listen. He asked me to sing in a talent show. I was dumfounded, but agreed
to try altho I'd probably die of stage fright. After our move to Arizona
and a large stage was built I fearfully made my singing debut. I received
nice compliments and unexpected attentions.
     The quiet, gentle and nice boys were afraid to approach me. Instead I
met the brash and bold ones. Among them was a shy, but loud young man.
Setsuji Okumoto was unsure of himself but determined to woo me. I was taken
aback by his bold proposal of marriage, but I liked his courage and direct
approach. Also his friend Thomas was a very intelligent, humorous and a
real gentleman. His word that Charlie (Setsuji) was a good boy carried
weight for I had a lot of respect for Thomas. I felt deep down there was a
lonely and love starved individual in Setsuji. It brought out a feeling of
kinship for I had gone thru moments of terrible loneliness in my days too.

One paragraph: Set-chan Proposal in Gila River Camp

played "go" on weekends with a friend. Four years later he had a fatal heart
attack and he joined mother and the house became terribly empty.
     Sadly I recalled the stories of their lives and I thought about them.
Father whose parents had such high hopes for him. Expecting him to become
a great soldier or navy man. His ancestors had been warriors of notable
worth. Because his grades in English had been poor his father sent him to
America to study. He certainly did not expect him to live the rest of his
life in America, for he must continue the Kawakita family tradition and name.
Having tasted his freedom, no strict ties, uncomfortable traditions, and
obligations, father was determined never to return to such a restricted
life. When he married my mother his family did not recognise her as his
wife for she was not of the right class of family . Yet right after the
war when Japan had a shortage of food, goods and medicene, mother sent them
needed articles and at last they welcomed her into their family.

One paragraph: Father Kawakita Funeral After Thoughts

Tome's 1942 Bride's Book

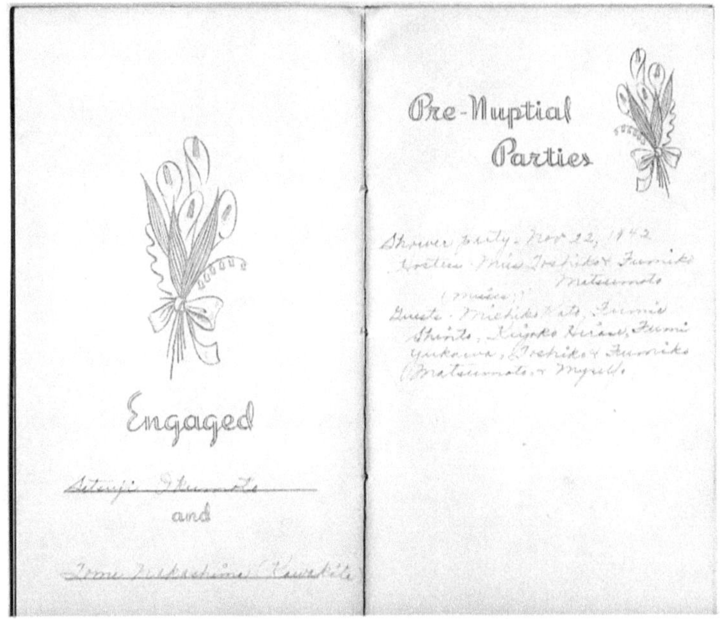

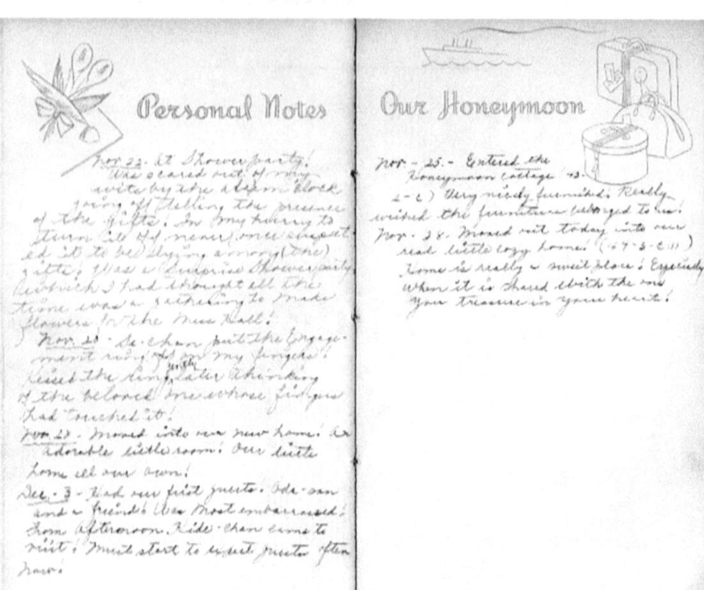
Personal Notes
Our Honeymoon

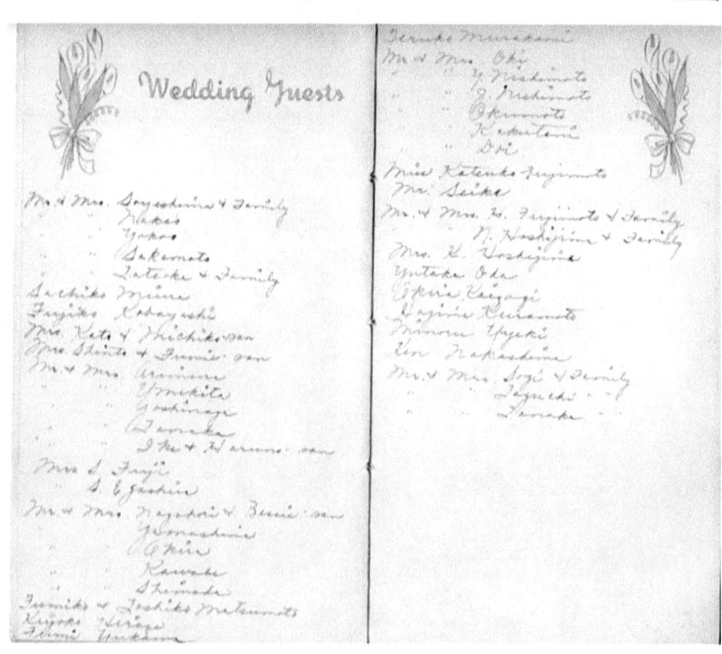
Wedding Guests

Handwritten Notes from Friends

Documents

A monetary sum and words alone cannot restore lost years or erase painful memories; neither can they fully convey our Nation's resolve to rectify injustice and to uphold the rights of individuals. We can never fully right the wrongs of the past. But we can take a clear stand for justice and recognize that serious injustices were done to Japanese Americans during World War II.

In enacting a law calling for restitution and offering a sincere apology, your fellow Americans have, in a very real sense, renewed their traditional commitment to the ideals of freedom, equality, and justice. You and your family have our best wishes for the future.

Sincerely,

GEORGE BUSH
PRESIDENT OF THE UNITED STATES

OCTOBER 1990

Letter of Apology to Tome from President George H. W. Bush

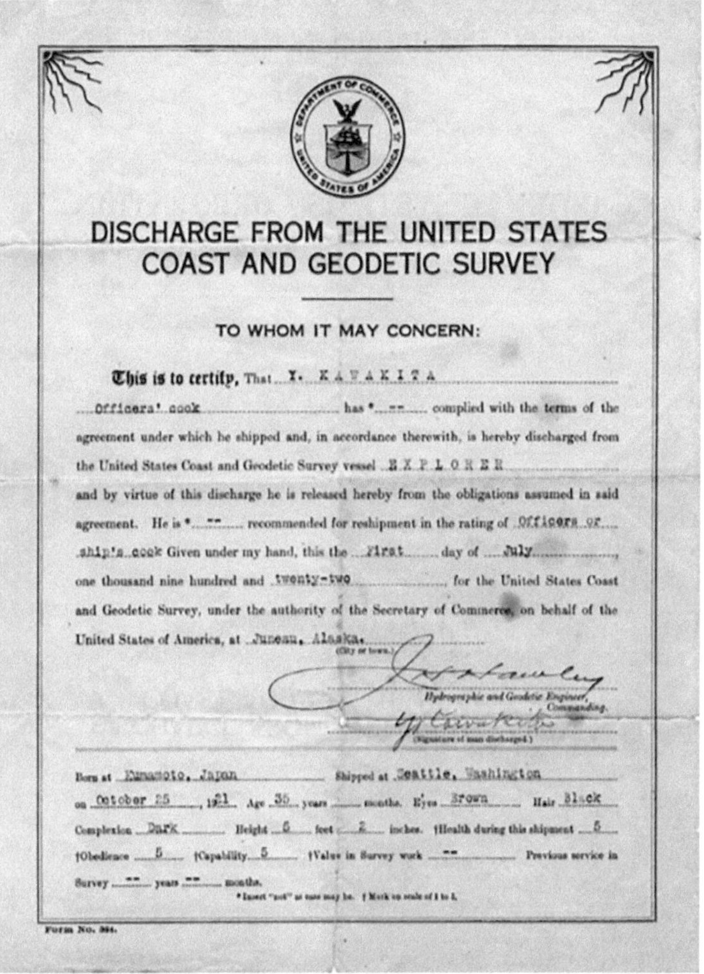

Father Kawakita 1922 Discharge from the Ship *Explorer*

As filed with the Securities and Exchange Commission on September 3, 1993

Registration No. 33-

SECURITIES AND EXCHANGE COMMISSION

Washington, D.C. 20549

Form S-1

REGISTRATION STATEMENT

Under

THE SECURITIES ACT OF 1933

CREDENCE SYSTEMS CORPORATION

(Exact name of Registrant as specified in charter)

Delaware	3825	94-287-8499
(State of incorporation)	(Primary Standard Industrial Classification Code Number)	(I.R.S. Employer Identification No.)

3500 West Warren Avenue
Fremont, California 94538
(510) 657-7400

(Address, including ZIP code, and telephone number, including area code, of Registrant's principal executive offices)

Elwood H. Spedden
President and Chief Executive Officer
Credence Systems Corporation
3500 West Warren Avenue
Fremont, California 94538
(510) 657-7400

(Name, address, including ZIP code, and telephone number, including area code, of agent for service)

Copies to:

Robert V. Gunderson, Jr., Esq.	William D. Sherman, Esq.
Warren T. Lazarow, Esq.	Christine A. Tomomatsu, Esq.
Jeffrey Y. Suto, Esq.	Karen A. Madsen, Esq.
Winnie Van, Esq.	Morrison & Foerster
Brobeck, Phleger & Harrison	755 Page Mill Road
Two Embarcadero Place	Palo Alto, California 94304
Palo Alto, California 94303	(415) 813-5600
(415) 424-0160	

Approximate date of commencement of proposed sale to the public:
As soon as practicable after the Registration Statement becomes effective and the Underwriting Agreement is executed.

If any of the securities being registered on this Form are to be offered on a delayed or continuous basis pursuant to Rule 415 under the Securities Act of 1933 check the following box: ☐

CALCULATION OF REGISTRATION FEE

Title of Each Class of Securities to be Registered	Amount to be Registered(1)	Proposed Maximum Offering Price per Share(2)	Proposed Maximum Aggregate Offering Price(2)	Amount of Registration Fee
Common Stock, $0.001 par value per share	2,875,000 shares	$16.00	$46,000,000	$14,375

(1) Includes 375,000 shares that the Underwriters have the option to purchase to cover over-allotments, if any.

(2) Estimated solely for the purpose of computing the amount of the registration fee pursuant to Rule 457(a).

The Registrant hereby amends this Registration Statement on such date or dates as may be necessary to delay its effective date until the Registrant shall file a further amendment which specifically states that this Registration Statement shall thereafter become effective in accordance with Section 8(a) of the Securities Act of 1933 or until the Registration Statement shall become effective on such date as the Commission, acting pursuant to said Section 8(a), may determine.

Credence S-1 Initial Public Offering (IPO): CFO Richard Y. Okumoto

MANAGEMENT

Directors, Executive Officers and Key Employees

The directors, executive officers and key employees of the Company, and their ages and positions as of July 31, 1993, are as follows:

Name	Age	Position
Directors and Executive Officers		
Wilmer R. Bottoms(1)(2)	50	Chairman of the Board of Directors
Elwood H. Spedden	56	President, Chief Executive Officer and Director
James T. Healy	53	Executive Vice President, Chief Operating Officer and Director
Richard Y. Okumoto	41	Senior Vice President, Chief Financial Officer and Secretary
Jos C. Henkens(1)	41	Director
Robert F. Kibble(2)	50	Director
Thomas E. Mees	36	Director
Bernard V. Vonderschmitt(2)	69	Director
Key Employees:		
Richard C. Carmichael	44	Senior Vice President, Marketing
Robert E. Huston	52	Senior Vice President, Test Technology
Gary J. Lesmeister	52	Chief Scientist
David M. O'Brien	36	Senior Vice President, Engineering
David A. Ranhoff	38	Senior Vice President, Sales

(1) Member of the Audit Committee

(2) Member of the Compensation Committee

Wilmer R. Bottoms has served on the Company's Board of Directors since 1985, was appointed acting Chairman of the Board in July 1991 and became Chairman of the Board in May 1992. Since 1984, Dr. Bottoms has been a *General Partner* and Senior Vice President of Patricof & Co. Ventures, Inc., a venture capital firm. From 1981 to 1984, Dr. Bottoms was President of the Semiconductor Equipment Group and Vice President of Varian Associates. Dr. Bottoms serves on the boards of directors of several private companies. See "Certain Relationships and Related Transactions."

Elwood H. Spedden has served as Chief Executive Officer and a Director since July 1991, and as President since August 1993. Between August 1990 and July 1991, Mr. Spedden served as Senior Vice President, Sales of the Company. From February 1989 to August 1990, Mr. Spedden served as Vice President, Sales of the Company. From September 1988 to February 1989, Mr. Spedden was a consultant for Telic Consulting Services. From December 1971 to September 1988, Mr. Spedden held a number of sales and marketing management positions with Teradyne, a semiconductor ATE manufacturer. Mr. Spedden also held various marketing and sales management positions with Hewlett-Packard Company, a computer and test equipment manufacturer. During the period from 1959 to 1967, Mr. Spedden was a designer of satellite telemetry systems with the Applied Physics Laboratory of the Johns Hopkins University.

James T. Healy has served as Executive Vice President since August 1993, and Chief Operating Officer and Director of the Company since July 1991. From July 1991 to August 1993, Mr. Healy was President of the Company. From December 1990 to July 1991, Mr. Healy served as Vice President and General Manager of the Fremont Division of the Company. Prior to joining the Company, Mr. Healy was a co-founder and served as President of Trilium Corporation ("Trilium"), a semiconductor test manufacturer, from 1982 to 1986. In 1986, Trilium merged with LTX, a semiconductor test manufacturer, and Mr. Healy became Senior Vice President, Corporate Marketing and Engineering and served in that position until December 1990. Mr. Healy was also Director of Operations for GenRad Semiconductor Test, Inc. ("GenRad") from March

---

Index

Index

Index

About the Author

RICHARD Y. OKUMOTO is a Silicon Valley executive, academic, and author whose life bridges cultures, generations, and disciplines. Born to a mother incarcerated in a WWII Japanese American internment camp and adopted by samurai, he rose from poverty and prejudice to earn a PhD from Queensland University of Technology, an MA from Gonzaga University, an MBA from Boston University, and a BS from San Jose State University. He is a former public-company CFO and whistleblower whose story, where the CEO pleaded guilty to accounting fraud, was captured in a Harvard Business Education case study, *The Midnight Journal Entry.*

Okumoto is a trained qualitative researcher who brings moral courage and analytical insight into his writings. He lives Bushido through his childhood lessons and as a black-belt trained in the traditional *Budo* philosophy of martial arts under Ken Funakoshi, a relative to the founder of modern karate, Gichin Funakoshi.

As a faculty member at San Jose State University, California State University–Long Beach, and the Keck Graduate Institute at Claremont Colleges, he has mentored future thought leaders while exploring the human dimensions of ethics, resilience, and purpose.